Beginner's Final Cut Pro

LEARN TO EDIT DIGITAL VIDEO

MICHAEL RUBIN

Peachpit
Press

Beginner's Final Cut Pro

Michael Rubin
Copyright ©2003 by Michael Rubin

Peachpit Press
1249 Eighth Street
Berkeley, CA 94710
510/524-2178
510/524-2221 (fax)

Find us on the World Wide Web at www.peachpit.com
To report errors, please send a note to errata@peachpit.com

Peachpit Press is a division of Pearson Education
©2001 *Song of Santa Cruz* mural by James Carl Aschbacher
©2000 "David (151)" written and performed by Suzanne Brewer. Used with permission.
Video clips and sketches ©2002 by Michael Rubin. Used with permission. May not be reproduced without written permission of the publisher.
Excerpts from *Nonlinear*, 4th edition, Triad Publishing Co. ©2000 Michael Rubin. Used with permission.

Editor: Kate McKinley
Production Coordinator: Lisa Brazieal
Copyeditor: John Tomasic
Compositor: Hugh D'Andrade, Jerry Ballew
Indexer: Emily Glossbrenner
Cover design: Seventeenth Street Studios
Interior design: Mimi Heft, Hugh D'Andrade

ISBN 0-321-11802-2

9 8 7 6 5 4 3 2

Printed and bound in the United States of America

Acknowledgments

This book reflects a method of editing education that evolved from the way I demonstrated and taught nonlinear editing systems from 1984 through 1992—from the EditDroid to the Avid/1. Filmmakers and editors were skeptical of those early tools, and were demanding about understanding the basic editing functionality minus the bells and whistles used to sell products. My deepest thanks to the great editors whom I trained and who trained me, in particular the mentoring of Gabriella Cristiani.

Also a sincere toast to the often-unrecognized teams of engineers who invented and designed the first few generations of nonlinear editing systems. I raise my glass to my compadres at Lucasfilm/The Droid Works and later at CMX. The widespread adoption of nonlinear editing today is vindication of much of our efforts back then.

Like all my video books, this also owes its roots to *Nonlinear,* the first textbook on digital editing, and my decade-long exercise in liberating postproduction from the clutches of an earlier century. The many people who supported and contributed to *Nonlinear* were supporters of this book as well, in particular Ron Diamond, Dean Godshall, Ken Yas, and Lisa Brenneis. And always, to Mary Sauer and Steve Arnold, who brought me into "the business" in the first place.

This book, like most of my works, relied on the trust and cooperation of my friends and family. A hearty thanks to Chris and Kirsten Mehl for volunteering to star in a soon-to-be classic scene; Chris Bryant for his BMX excellence and FCP enthusiasm; Lisa Strong-Aufhauser for her valuable production contributions; Suzanne Brewer, for her fine music; and to Lisa Jensen and James Carl Aschbacher; Danny, Louise, Maida, and Asa Rubin; and Ian and Olivia Elman.

Thanks to the team at Peachpit Press who all seem to tolerate my unorthodox visions and guide me into acceptably professional books in the process: my editor and sometime-therapist Kate McKinley; the watchful guidance of Becky Morgan; and the maternal discipline of Marjorie Baer. Also a hearty thank you to the rest of the book team at Peachpit: Nancy Ruenzel, Gary-Paul Prince, Scott Cowlin, Mimi Heft, Lisa Brazieal, and all the rest.

A quick hug and kiss to the extended Rubin family—in Toronto, Santa Fe, Gainesville, Sedona, New York, and wherever they roam. I want to specially send love to my parents for their ongoing enthusiasm and interest in my disparate ventures.

Finally, the true source and inspiration for this book—Jennifer and Jonah, whose lives are so a part of my own that any work of mine necessitates their profound tolerance and unwavering support. Jen, it grows truer and truer: At the end of the day, all this technology isn't really worth squat.

—Michael Rubin

Contents

Introduction

I like Final Cut Pro. I waited for years before I could own an editing system at home that was as good as those I used professionally. It arrived in 1998 and I've been pretty busy since then.

There are plenty of great books on the details and features of FCP. This book doesn't replace those; it is not designed to teach you *everything* about Final Cut Pro. It won't familiarize you with all the cool features, and it won't make you an expert.

This book is designed for **beginners**—beginners to editing, perhaps, and beginners to Final Cut Pro. My goal is to take you from novice to skilled editor on the shortest possible path. You will acquire the skills of an excellent editor, you will edit a scene from a movie (well, I'm using the term loosely), and you will learn all the *whats, whys, wheres,* and *hows* of making your own videos. And you will understand the core functions of Final Cut Pro.

Final Cut Pro is a professional-level tool. It can be used to make commercials, corporate videos, television programs, and even feature films. Its many sophisticated functions are available to you as your skills and interests develop. But there is one thing I want to impress upon you: **Editing is simple.**

This is a professional film editing tool:

It's called a cutting block. You use it to hold the film in position while a razor blade swings down and neatly chops the film into two pieces. In one form or another, the cutting block has been used in Hollywood for more than 100 years, and it's a powerful yet simple device. Editing *is* simple. So is Final Cut Pro. You don't need all the power and features of FCP to edit.

My Method

Most FCP training takes you methodically through all the features of the product, and introduces you to the myriad ways they can be executed. I teach a wholly different approach that isn't so concerned with numbers and typing, with speed and the computer interface. I try to focus on the video material itself and what you want to do with it.

Final Cut Pro easily accomodates this style, but it might seem strange to people who have never edited film, or who are deeply entrenched in the wonderful features of a Mac with FCP. I've edited in this nonlinear style exclusively since 1985; I came to an appreciation of nonlinear editing through its evolution as a hybrid of both film and video. As a student (and teacher) of computerized editing, I find that explanations that use real-world objects as their metaphor are very logical and comprehensible. Editing film really means cutting and taping real things together, and because it has form in the physical world it is its own graphical interface. I think this makes it easy to understand.

In my approach many seemingly important FCP features will be skimmed over or ignored completely, because I only want you to concentrate on the concept and tool at hand. I gloss over keyboard equivalents, I ignore manual entry of time-codes, I refer to certain features by their conceptual name and not their FCP user manual name, and it may even seem that I present functions in a disorderly fashion. We edit in Chapter 2, and we won't learn about media files or capturing until Chapter 5—completely backward from virtually every other text.

I believe you'll learn faster this way and ultimately have a deeper understanding of Final Cut Pro and all editing in the end.

The Ultimate Oxymoron: *Beginner's* FCP

Isn't iMovie the proper beginner's product? Wouldn't anyone using FCP be a pro already?

It's true: FCP is designed for professionals. It provides all the tools a professional would need, with an interface similar to those found on other professional products. It will be there for you as your interest and skills expand, but it is also easy to ignore many of the features and just focus on the basics. I think FCP is actually *easier* than many consumer-oriented editing products.

Who I Am

I've been assisting editors and editing my own projects for many years, editing TV shows, Hollywood movies, commercials, and an occasional music video. I was involved with the invention and revolution of computerized editing systems. My first job was working for George Lucas, the man whose pioneering work in developing nonlinear editing has been largely eclipsed by some of his flashier and more lucrative accomplishments. In 1991 I wrote the first book in the field—*Nonlinear.* Now in its fourth edition, it's the classic used by students and professionals in computer, video, and film.

Oddly enough, I don't consider my years in the professional industry my greatest credential. Perhaps more importantly, I've spent four years shooting and editing my own personal videos with Final Cut Pro. I learned a creative workflow with short, efficient schedules (my wife is a tougher producer than any I worked for in Hollywood) and that process is the substance of what I bring to this book.

Finally, I truly enjoy teaching and sharing. I believe the revolution that's brewing is not about encouraging everyone to make Hollywood movies (although that's fun), but rather giving the skills of video and editing to a generation that can apply them in whatever unique and personal ways they choose—for work or for play.

What You Need

The only things you really need to use this book are any version of Final Cut Pro software, a Mac that will run it, and some footage to play with. That's it.

We're going to be learning the very core fundamentals of Final Cut, and these basics haven't changed much at all from version 1 to version 3. The great thing about fundamentals is, they're so...*fundamental.*

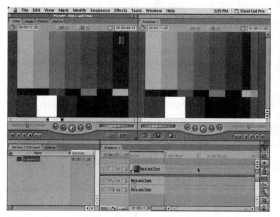 

FCP version 1 on left, version 3 on right. Need I say more?

Let me put it this way. If you have any version at all of FCP running on your Mac, you're good to go. If you don't already have FCP up and running, your first assignment is to make sure the software can run on your Mac (check the current version's memory and hardware requirements if you have questions), and install it.

Footage. This book is about video, so you're going to need some footage to play with to follow along. If you're going to edit, you really do need either a DV or Digital8 camera and some footage of your own. But for using this book, you only need a DVD drive on your Mac so you can use the enclosed tutorial footage.

You may feel a certain longing, an urge, to jump right into these editing tools using your *own* video, ignoring the typically dull tutorial content provided. I feel your pain. But you need to play around with certain *kinds* of material to properly understand many of these tools and editing concepts.

What I Have

I recently bought a dual GHz G4 with OS X, but I also own a 500 MHz G3 iBook laptop, which I use to edit for classes and on the road. The reason I use the iBook and not the top-of-the-line Titanium PowerBook is only that it dramatically makes the point to beginning editors that you don't need the most expensive computer or the newest, fastest CPUs. Today every new Apple is plenty good to edit with FCP. Even the entry-level iMac comes with a fast and powerful 700 MHz G4 CPU, and in time you can be sure this will be upgraded. Honestly, you could learn FCP—and follow along with this book—using version 2 on an older G3. It's not ideal, but it would work.

I am writing and illustrating this book using FCP 3 in both OS 9.2.2 and OS 10.1.2—but the cold reality is that I could have written 99 percent of it using FCP 2 in OS 9.1, or even FCP 1 in OS 8.5. The basics are the basics. The interface hasn't changed much and the core tools have been there since day one and will probably still be there in version 4. Some menus get shuffled a little, but in general, all the features you need are going to be right where I say they are and work the way I say they work, regardless of operating system or software version.

The most important reason to use a high-end Mac to do video has mostly to do with speed; that is, how fast these computers can render complex special effects (which I hardly ever need) and how quickly they can burn DVDs (which I now do occasionally). These are reasons to consider using Macs at the higher end of the food chain, but editing isn't. Also, a nice big hard drive is important (and two can improve performance), but you're fine if you have more than 20 GB—and I doubt you can even *get* a Mac today with less than 40 GB.

I first learned about editing playing with 20 minutes of video from Scene 50 of *Return of the Jedi*. That just happened to be the material Lucasfilm chose in 1984 to illustrate the power of its groundbreaking EditDroid nonlinear editing system. No lightsabers or X-wing fighters. In fact, no fancy special effects at all. A simple back-and-forth dialog scene between Yoda and Luke Skywalker.

I provide about 20 minutes of video clips on the enclosed DVD-ROM. While this scene does not have the hip cachet of something from *Star Wars*, I designed it purely to provide a workzone featuring the most common editing situations. Real personal video is unscripted and will be wholly unlike this kind of material. Yet the scripted scenes provided here make all the subtleties of editing easily visible, and will likely teach you more than you could imagine about shooting your videos and telling a story through editing.

Where We're Headed

The editing skills we learn here apply equally to either professional or personal video. When we're done, assuming you pay attention, you will:

- Understand the basic technical stuff about video and your computer
- Know hwow to capture video quickly
- Know how to organize your video materials efficiently
- Be able to insert, arrange, and trim your clips into a storyline
- Be able to add a touch of polish, like transition effects, music, and titles
- Know how to output your final movie to videotape, the Web, and DVD

So roll up your sleeves, pull up a chair, and let's learn how to use FCP to edit videos, even if you never cut anything more professional than a baby video or a birthday party. And just keep thinking of that cutting block. Great tools don't have to be complicated to be powerful.

This is going to be fun.

CHAPTER 1 # First Things First

Before we start capturing and editing and maybe getting ourselves hopelessly confused, I want to take you on my personal tour of Final Cut Pro. In particular, we'll break down what you see on the screen (the *interface*) into understandable components.

Before the interface tour begins, however, I'll walk you through the most critical aspect of any editing tool: control over how you move and play the video. By the end of this chapter, you'll be on a first-name basis with the FCP interface; it will be familiar and comfortable, and you'll be ready to learn to edit.

FCP and Post-Production

Shooting, organizing, and editing are generally seen as distinct tasks, although in truth they often blur and meld together—I think of the combination as "holistic video." No matter how good an editor you are or how skilled you are with editing software, it's almost impossible to have a positive editing experience with really poorly shot video. And even if you're the best videographer in the world, all that matters in the end is the product edited from your raw material. Shooting and editing are *yin* and *yang*—independent and yet intertwined. (Forgive me, I moved to California a number of years ago, and this kind of New Age metaphor has finally lodged itself in my thinking.)

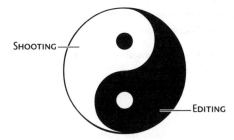

This is a book about "post-production"—by definition, the things that happen to a film after it is shot. For us, post-production includes three steps:

- Getting raw "source" video into your computer ("capturing it")
- Editing the video
- Outputting the finished cut sequence to a "master" videotape

Final Cut Pro manages all of these tasks. There are, however, other post-production tasks worth noting. At the front end of post-production I think it is important to create a *logsheet* outlining the material on a given videotape "reel." Editors usually log video right before or while they're capturing it. At the back end of the process, there are a number of output options available using FCP. I end this book with a section detailing how to record your final edits to a master digital video cassette, but many of you will want to have a compressed QuickTime version for use on the

Web, and you may want to burn a DVD. Creating these versions involves time-consuming (and computationally complex) software compression of your video. That compression produces lower-quality video than the DV video you started with. Once you have a high-quality digital videotape *master*, it is up to you what other formats you want to create, but I think it is critical to view the output of the master as the most significant "final" step of post-production.

VOCABULARY: Master

The word master is used in special ways throughout the filmmaking process, which sometimes can be a little confusing.

1 **NOUN** The final version of an edited sequence.

2 **NOUN** The dedicated video monitor on which you watch the master (see 1). This "master" display is also sometimes called the "record" monitor. In this case, master is the opposite of source.

3 **NOUN** The main shot of a particular scene, as recorded during production. The master (shot) tends to run the entire length of a scene, and is often—but not always—a wide shot. A scene may include a master and a series of closer shots.

4 **NOUN** A tape or device from which the timecode drives other devices (known as "slaves") such that all devices are held in synchronization.

5 **VERB** To record the final version to an ultimate destination. People often master music files, for example, when they burn them on a CD-R device.

It would not be unusual, therefore, to say something like: "I noticed that my *master* (shot) dominates the edited *master* (version) that I am watching on my *master* (monitor) while I *master (record)* the project." *Whew.* (I take it back: Saying that would be a little unusual.)

Your "Edit Bay"

With little more than a Mac and DV camera, you can pretty much edit anywhere—I've edited in airport terminals and sitting in my car waiting for a meeting. An *edit bay* is a place set up to facilitate editing. Primarily, it includes three things: a Mac, a digital camcorder, and a FireWire cable. It might also include a video display (or TV), a comfy chair, a box of videotapes, and a log book. When you're souping up your bay, you might add a nice set of speakers and perhaps a dedicated digital video cassette player. But we're going to start simple: camcorder, Mac, FCP. Minimum configuration.

We won't be capturing video this early in the book, so you can launch FCP with or without your camera connected.

Still, let's go through the steps to make sure you understand how to hook up your camera and Mac. You'll need a 4-pin to 6-pin FireWire cable.

The smaller side (the 4-pin side) slides into your camera.

The larger side (6-pin "D") plugs into the Mac.

Unlike hooking up car battery jumper cables it really doesn't matter which end you plug in first. What's more, FireWire is designed to be "hot swappable," which means you can plug things in even when your computer is running (in the old days of SCSI, you had to turn everything off before messing with the cabling; this is a fine advancement).

While FCP can be made to look around anytime to see if you've plugged in any new "hot swapped" devices, it is my habit to plug in hardware before I launch the application. It seems to cut down on problems.

This is what it looks like as you hook up your camera to your computer:

1 Plug the small end of your FireWire cable into your camera.

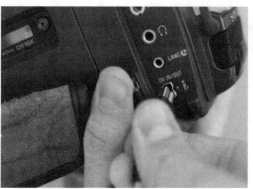

2 Plug the larger end of the FireWire cable into your Mac.

With your camera and Mac connected, and your camera turned on (and set to VCR mode), you are ready to launch your application and get down to biz.

A Video Monitor

For all but the most basic set-up, a video monitor is really essential. You can certainly edit without one, and if you want the smallest possible configuration, by all means, skip it, but in no time you'll realize that video doesn't look "right" on a computer display. In general, it simply *can't*. Video plays on TVs in completely different ways than it does on computers. Without getting overly technical, let's just agree that FCP can't play your video smoothly and sharply in its interface, and even when it's playing as well as it can, you're still watching it in a little window.

And thus the problem: To make good editing decisions, you really need to see video in the *way it will be ultimately viewed.* If something is shot for the big screen of a movie theater, you really need to see it played in a theater. Same with home video. While it's easy to watch your video on the Mac display, or even mirrored on the LCD display of your (connected) DV camera, the ideal way to edit is to take the video signal from FCP and pump it to a television set. This allows you to see the motion, the size, the colors, the framing, as it will look once translated from digital video signal to analog signal—the way it will be when played on a typical television.

Connecting this up is easy, even for me.

Monitors and TVs

To be fair, a television is not really the same thing as a video monitor, although I tend to use the terms interchangeably here. And while we're on the topic, a video monitor is not interchangeable with a computer monitor. The most important difference for us concerns the available plugs on the back (or maybe front) of the display. Monitors designed to display video have an array of input/output plugs (analog, S-Video, and so forth); televisions do not, and sometimes sport only a single RF (coaxial) knobby for connecting up the cable. When you're just starting out, I wouldn't bother purchasing a dedicated monitor; you can get by with an old TV set, which can often be found for cheap or even free.

This Is How I Hook Up a TV

Method 1: Analog Cables Since I usually have my camera hooked up to my computer with the FireWire cable, all I do to see my video on a TV is take the analog output of my camera (using either the S-Video plug or the simple composite analog video/audio plug) and just jack those into any regular TV.

Here's how I plug in the analog cables. This gives me both video (the yellow plug) and stereo audio (the red and white plugs for left and right):

1 Plug the special RCA-mini plug (a.k.a. the ¼-inch plug) into the audio/video jack on your camera. It probably doesn't say "analog input or output" but this is what it is.

2 Plug the three RCA plugs into your video monitor. They likely will be labeled Video and Audio.

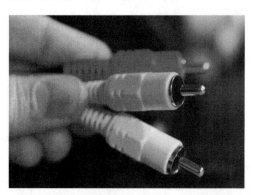

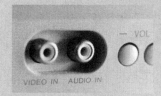

Some TVs only have a mono input for audio—one plug—and so you must either (1) plug in only one of the two stereo inputs (the red or the white); or (2) get a stereo-to-mono adapter (sometimes called a Y-cord) that will let you push the red and white plugs into one side and then connect the single plug on the other side to your TV.

Method 2: S-Video If you want to use the (higher quality) S-Video signal for the picture, plug an S-Video cable into the camera and into the S-Video input on your monitor (Note: Not all monitors have an S-Video input). Remember that the S-Video cable carries only video and doesn't carry audio, so you'll still need the audio signal (using the connection I described above). Simply unplug the (yellow) video plug, but leave the (red and white) audio cables connected. It looks weird, but it's OK to have the video cable hanging there. If you're particularly fastidious, you could use a different cable that has no yellow audio component, but I don't think it's worth buying a separate cable.

1 Plug the S-Video cable into the camera.

2 Plug the other end into the monitor (both ends are the same, so it doesn't matter which way this goes).

3 Remove the video plug from the analog set-up, and leave it dangling!

Method 3: With a VCR There are a few reasons you might want to insert a regular old VCR (probably VHS) in the middle of all this TV cabling.

First, your TV may not have the S-Video or analog RCA plugs we've been talking about. But even the cheapest old television has a plug for cable service. (This type of plug is known as an RF type, and the cable is called coaxial cable.) The easiest way to get from the camera to the TV with only an RF connector is to put a VCR in the middle:

1 Plug your camera into the VCR as if it were the TV in methods 1 and 2.

2 Run a coaxial cable from the VCR output to the TV.

The second reason you might want to do this—even if your TV can be connected to the camera—is so you can make VHS dubs of material on your DV camera. Getting the VCR into the pathway facilitates this.

Loading in the Video Files

Traditionally, video material comes from a video shoot—in our case, from a digital camcorder. But as we delve into the basics of FCP, we're going to use video that I'm providing explicitly for this purpose. This material is the patient and you are the doctor. (OK, well, maybe the material is the cadaver, and you're the medical student...whatever.) We're going to learn about editing, the tools you need, and the nuances of the art, using very standard, simple material.

Let's begin by getting the video from the DVD into your Mac.

1 Insert the DVD that came with this book.

2 Locate the folder labeled "Rubin's Tutorial Files."

> If you're putting it on your desktop—as opposed to on a particular hard drive—remember to hold down the Option key while you click-drag-release or else the file will not be copied and when you remove the DVD the folder will disappear!

3 Drag the entire folder to your hard disk. This will copy the entire contents to your Mac and you can take out the DVD and put it away for safekeeping. It doesn't matter where you put the folder on your hard disk, just be sure to remember where you drop it. Since it won't be here forever, I like to put it right on the desktop, where it's easier to find and easier to delete.

A Tour Through the Interface

Your computer screen, whether 12 or 20 inches across, must contain all the various windows and icons required to edit. Can it be done? Certainly. Some windows must be visible pretty much all the time; others you only need to check out once in awhile, so you'll tuck them away neatly and get back to them when the mood strikes.

Launch FCP

If you haven't done so already, launch FCP.

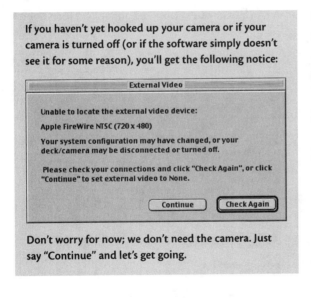

If you haven't yet hooked up your camera or if your camera is turned off (or if the software simply doesn't see it for some reason), you'll get the following notice:

External Video

Unable to locate the external video device:

Apple FireWire NTSC (720 x 480)

Your system configuration may have changed, or your deck/camera may be disconnected or turned off.

Please check your connections and click "Check Again", or click "Continue" to set external video to None.

Continue   Check Again

Don't worry for now; we don't need the camera. Just say "Continue" and let's get going.

One of the nifty features of FCP is that the screen, while cohesive and tight, is composed of a handful of distinct elements that can be moved around and resized to your personal preference. Of course, if you are new to FCP, you're not going to have much of a preference, and so we will begin with the format that is the default for the software. I don't think this presentation is ideal, but it's so dern close that we might as well start here before messing around with modifications.

Here's the display as it opens up in the standard default configuration (and on a typical monitor).

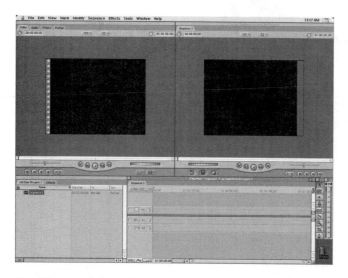

You'll notice that there are four sections of the display (plus a toolbox). Here they are disassembled:

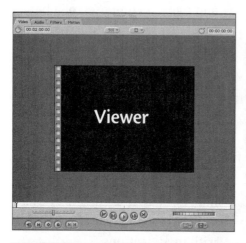

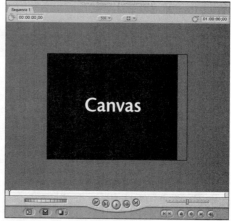

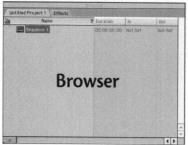

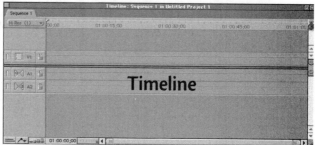

Now that you've seen them taken apart, let's put them back together and see what they are and how they work together.

Once you can recognize each individual window, you need to understand the concept of *window activation*. Many functions and menu options are only available from one window. To make a window the active one, simply click it. If you find you can't perform an action—say, controlling the Viewer or importing a clip—it may be because the wrong window is active. When in doubt, click the appropriate window before working.

The Browser

Your source material, which is the raw footage captured from your camera (or in our case, imported from a DVD), stacks up in the Browser, a box that contains all the materials of your project (but initially only the original footage). The Browser can display its contents in a variety of ways (as a text list, as picture icons, and so forth), but for now, let's keep the default format and just look at the Browser as a text list of clips:

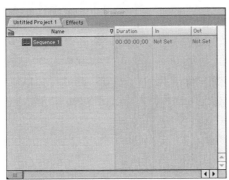

Notice there is only one item here (a "sequence," but don't worry about that now). This is how your Browser will look when you first start out.

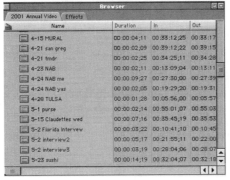

Compare this to the way a typical Browser appears in the middle of a bigger project. Although there are more things stacked up in the text list, it appears essentially the same as it did before.

The Viewer

The Viewer is where you watch your raw material; it's where you mark the frames at which shots begin and end. It is the jumping-off point for editing. The lowest part of the Viewer contains an assortment of play controls and functions. We'll investigate these controls later in this chapter, but for now, just note where they are.

The Canvas

For the moment, think of editing as finding bits of video in the Viewer and dragging those bits into the Canvas. While the Canvas has many special properties, it works pretty much the same as the Viewer. These little TV sets are the same *type* of device, with only some special features added that customize them for their respective tasks. On first glance, they look practically identical; but when you're talking about things in FCP, it's good to be able to distinguish the Viewer (source material) from the Canvas (cut material), and know the vocabulary. If you're ever unsure of what you're looking at, labels appear faintly at the top of each window.

Once something is cut into the Canvas, it's also cut into the Timeline. They're two views of the same object.

The Timeline

The Timeline is a classic graphical interface for editing that represents pieces of picture and sound cut together. Its strengths are twofold:

- It shows clips in lengths relative to each other, so at a glance you know a lengthy shot is going to take more time to play than a shorter shot.

- It shows you where edits between shots happen, relative to other edits in other tracks—mainly sound tracks that might be different from picture tracks.

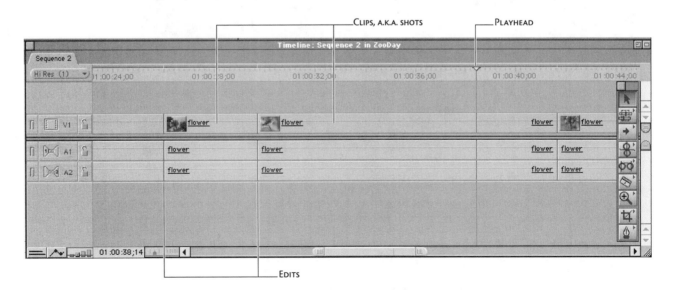

The Timeline is where you see the pictures that come together to form the apparently cohesive whole that plays in your Canvas. Dragging the playhead around on the Timeline will show you the video in the Canvas that corresponds to the playhead position. Add a transition in the Canvas, and you'll see the graphical display of the transition in the Timeline. Like I said, they go together.

Workflow

I think it's good to imagine these windows as a kind of cycle, to visualize material entering the wheel at bottom left, moving up, to the right, and down, like this:

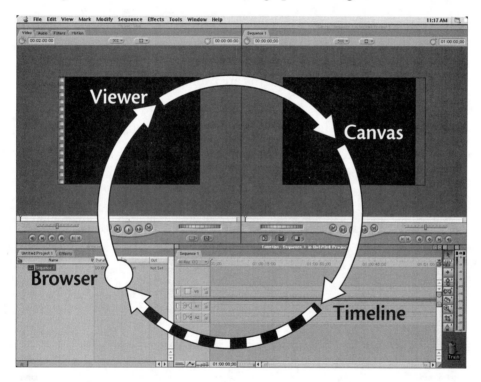

While there are notable exceptions to this flow, it is one way of looking at how these discrete windows work together. Another way is to think of the windows at the bottom of the screen as the *data* and the windows up top as the *media*, so editing is the process of moving material from the left side of the screen to the right. Either way, it amounts to about the same thing.

As we get into editing, remember these general kinds of flows.

FCP and Your Computer

When you launch FCP, a new project is opened, an unnamed and as-yet unsaved project, where you can work. This blank workspace looks like this on your display:

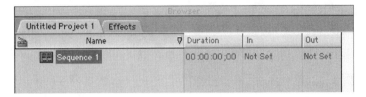

Projects consist of two fundamental types of things: clips and sequences. When you capture videotape from your camera, you are capturing *clips*. Like the video-

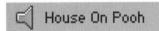

tape they came from, clips are usually combinations of video and audio, but they can be strictly video, represented by an icon that looks like this.

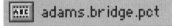

Or audio (like music or a voiceover), represented by an icon that looks like this.

You can also import still images in a variety of still-image formats (such as JPEG, GIF, and TIFF), which show up like this.

When you start editing, you're generally starting with raw clips and building them together into sequences. A sequence is created through a series of "edit decisions." When you open a project for the first time, there is always one empty sequence in the Browser already. And as you edit more, you will add new sequences as necessary. Here's the icon for a sequence:

Title Variations

Truck Cut

Whenever you open a project, the Browser will display a list of all the elements already there, a mixture of clips and sequences. It's important to be able to distinguish them at a glance.

Which ones are clips and which are sequences? Familiarize yourself with the icons.

Now, even though there's nothing here in this new untitled and unsaved project, let's go ahead and save the current project and give it a name.

1 Choose File > Save Project As.

A dialog box will appear, asking for a name for this project.

2 Type a name in the highlighted box. Might I suggest "My Tutorial Project"? (Feel free to improvise here.)

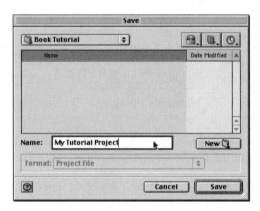

Once you've saved the project with a name, you will notice the interface is changed ever so slightly:

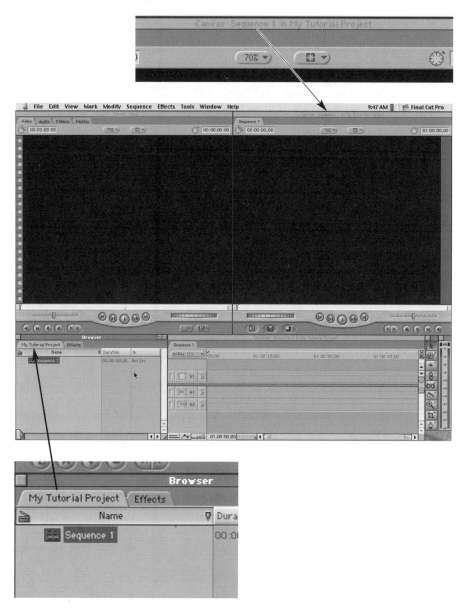

In faint type above the Canvas and Timeline, for instance, the name of the project has been updated. You'll also see a tab with this project's name on the Browser.

I name tape reels very methodically for organizational purposes, but I give project names a little more color and description, like "Zoo Day" or "Beach" or even "Triathlon 12-02." I've found that for my personal projects, the best names are descriptive.

Professional projects may require more functional project names, but for my home projects I have never had a problem with the more casual labels.

I think for now this is all you need to know about creating and saving a project. We'll spend more time exploring ways to organize files on your Mac once you've had some fun editing.

Importing Video Clips

Let's go get two clips from the Chapter 1 trutorial folder and put them into this new project. Leave the rest for now (as I don't want anything to be too confusing yet).

Go through these steps:

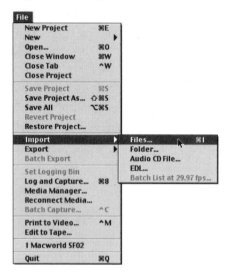

1 With the Browser active, choose File > Import > Files.

2 Select VidClip1 and press Enter (or click Open).

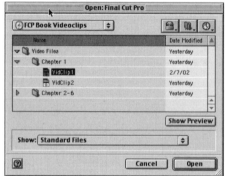

Repeat these steps for VidClip2.

Now that these two clips are in your Browser, let's take them out for a drive.

This has nothing to do with capturing video from a camera—your principle method of getting material into FCP. Importing the tutorial video is more like importing still images from other folders on your Mac or moving clips from one project into another. You can read all about what we're doing here in a good reference guide, but as far as I'm concerned, it's OK to just get through it; it really doesn't come up that often in beginning to edit on FCP.

Playtime

I'm not a power user. I know lots of power users and I think they're cool, but I never have much time to learn a lot of editing shortcuts. Consequently, I don't edit as quickly as is *possible*. It doesn't bother me. Editing is more than speed in executing commands. Professionals benefit greatly from working exceptionally fast, but I haven't found speed as important an editing skill in my personal video work. Shortcuts will come in time, as you find your own style for working the controls.

If you use a mouse with great dexterity, you might do *everything* with the mouse. Open files, play video, shuttle around. Grab tools and make edits. I think this is a good way for a beginner to first experience many of the editing tools—I started this way. You can do this, but from time to time you will still need the simple hunt-and-peck for an odd keyboard item.

And as time goes on, you realize that some tasks are easier (or more logical) to perform with your fingers on the keys and some are perfectly easy with a mouse.

Playspeed vs. Nonplay Speed

Press Play on any VCR, CD deck, or other audio or video device, and the machine runs at "playspeed." *Fast forward* and *fast reverse* are examples of "nonplay speeds," as they are moving the media in unusual directions and velocities. When you edit, you will learn to live with video and audio played at many nonplay speeds (from very slow creeping or stepping, to high-speed scanning), all of which are important depending on what you are doing. Playspeed reverse, a special case where the video moves in normal playspeed but backward, provides almost as much information to the editor as the more familiar forward direction.

Method I: One Hand on Mouse

Let's start with the mouse. Use one hand (your mouse hand), and let's do it *all* this way.

 First, double-click VidClip1 in the Browser to open it into the Viewer. At the bottom of the Viewer you'll see a row of controls for playing the video. The bottom of the Canvas has the same controls, and they work just the same

Play

Click on the Play button in the Viewer and your video will start to move forward, in "playspeed." While this seems like a pretty common need, it's actually only one way you'll want to see things. Notice that once you've clicked Play, if you click the button again the video stops. Start and stop your video a few times.

I don't use the Play button all that often.

Shuttle Knob

The shuttle knob is really my third-favorite controller (but it's the first one you should examine in detail). Holding onto one point (click and hold, drag left and right), I can go forward or backward, slow or fast. It is forgiving—if you're sloppy and your hand strays a little high or low in one direction or another, as long as you still have the click-and-hold secure, you'll pull that shot along in the appropriate direction. This is good. It gives me a feeling of acceleration as I head in one direction or another, and yet the video plays smoothly enough at the higher speeds to let me skim the footage.

You'll want to be reasonably familiar with the footage. Linearly shuttling through the tape at these super-high speeds allows you to find things that you didn't know you were going to be looking for. That's one of the special aspects of editing: As you work, you realize you need some certain shot to solve a problem, and now you know how to get that shot quickly to see if your instinct was right, to see if the shot works.

Perhaps the best thing about shuttling is that the audio pitch increases or decreases with speed; the material you're watching *sounds* slower or faster. It's a nice feedback for the user about speed and direction and can be useful in the rhythmic motions that are part of selecting a frame to edit.

The shuttle knob, while cool, is only so fast. In fact, at full crank it moves about 20X playspeed. It skips frames to move this fast, but you still see much of the action on the tape. (Most cameras, by the way, can only shuttle at 10X speed and still let you watch the video.)

When you're really racing around linearly, you want this next control.

> **Audio Scrub**
>
> There are two ways to hear sound moving at nonplay speeds. The first is with the pitch changing as the speed changes (a familiar sound from old analog editing days). The second (a nifty modern invention) holds the pitch constant regardless of the speed. The shuttle controller allows for the pitch change; moving slowly with the jog wheel, for instance, holds the pitch constant.

Scrubber Bar

I like this device. Under each video image (in the Viewer or Canvas) there is a horizontal bar—a graphical representation of the duration of the entire clip of video you are watching. It works in much the same way as the shuttle knob: click, hold, drag left or right (you can also just click somewhere within the length of the bar). The difference is that the bar is not scaled to speed, but scaled to length (position). Click all the way to the left and you're at the beginning of the clip. Click all the way to the right, and bam, you're at the end. It could be a 5-second clip or a 50-minute clip, you can zoom from the beginning to the end just by clicking, or clicking-and-dragging.

Thus, the longer the clip, the faster you move here (and the harder it is to "hit" any exact spot). For beginners, it's usually more difficult to negotiate the scrubber bar with long clips of, say, 10–20 minutes (clicking and dragging and stopping must be much more tightly coordinated); anything under 10 minutes is pretty basic to control, but if that's still too much, try less. The more skilled you are with this click-hold-drag motion, the longer your clip can be and still be really useful. Two- to ten-minute clips is a very manageable compromise in terms of capturing video. And it makes the scrubber bar pretty easy to use and thus a powerful ally.

Now, with this tool and the shuttle knob, you can pop around in the clip and scan at super high speed looking for something. When you're near what you're looking for, drop down to the shuttle knob, and pull back toward the shot. When you edit, finding a bit of video you like is about not only finding "it" but finding the *first frame* of it and the *last frame* of it. Those are not approximations, those are precise decisions and they matter. Being able to hit a particular frame is critical.

Ahh, but even these three methods, play, shuttle, and zoom-in-the-scrubber, are all too *macro*. What you always need is some *micro* manipulation. And thus, we come to....

The Jog Wheel

This is another device borrowed from professional videotape machines, where it doesn't quite "play" the videotape so much as "nudge" it forward or backward a bit at a time. This is called "jogging" and it's important. The jog wheel is open ended and loose; it rolls and rolls in whatever direction you click and drag. In some respects, it's like a finer-tuned shuttle knob. If you pull far from the center point, it will jog faster; small pulls from the center and you can move a gentle frame or two at a time.

There actually is a fourth excellent on-screen navigation tool. Simply grab the playhead in the Timeline and drag it around. This is actually my favorite method for bouncing around on screen, but it only works in the Timeline. I won't use it in this exercise, but we will use it as we get deeper into editing.

I don't use the jog wheel all that often (and I'll explain why after you've played with it).

Now you are ready to combine these on-screen play controls.

Target Practice

Double-click the VidClip1 icon in the Browser. This will open it up in the Viewer window right above it. You are now looking at the first frame of this clip. If you've been playing around in this clip already, use the scrubber bar now to move to the first frame.

I want you to shuttle through your clip and stop on the frame with the small white dot, called a *punch* in film editing. This task is a little easier than it might have been because you are making use of the clap, the audio "clue," so you have more senses working on the task.

Some Background

The clip is of a slate (or clapboard), a typical Hollywood device that both labels the following bit of film and provides the very functional purpose of allowing pictures to be synchronized with sound tracks. When a slate is snapped shut, there is one frame where the jaws are open and a next frame where the jaws are closed.

There is also a distinct spot in the sound track where there is no sound, and then there is the first frame of sound. Like a spike:

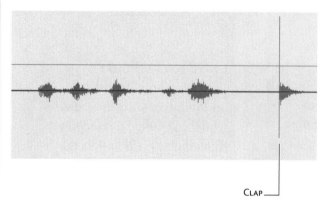

CLAP

When you line these two things up, picture and sound are in sync. (Another way to think about this is that they are lined up to start with, and if they ever accidentally moved out of sync through various procedures, they can be realigned.)

Of course, in the real world, sometimes the camera catches the jaws in a blur. And in this case, the clap happens sort of between two frames, no one frame is the precise and only sync spot, and thus the person whose job it is to synchronize these elements simply chooses one.

When the correct frame of picture is identified, to make it easy to find again (particularly if it's unclear), it is marked, typically with a hole punch. This punch produces a kind of "flash" as you play through a reel of film and is relatively easy to find. It is one frame long, which means it flashes on the screen for $1/30$th of a second—0.033 seconds or 3.3 tenths of a second. You'd be surprised how short that is. You'd be surprised how long it can be.

Try different methods, but always using the mouse.

- The Play and Stop button
- The shuttle knob
- The scrubber bar
- The jog wheel
- A combination of them, as desired, for accuracy

When this seems easy enough, you might try again with the sound off, just to make sure you're using your eyes and not your ears. In real editing, sometimes you will use both, but just as often you're searching with only your eyes or only your ears. You won't go wrong practicing with each.

Of all these on-screen motion controls, the one I have the biggest problem with is the jog wheel. Sometimes you just need to move one frame, and it's actually a fair amount of work to do with the jog wheel. And so I end up heading for the keyboard. And once you have your fingers on the keyboard, a new horizon opens up in the land of video navigation.

Method 2: One Hand on the Keyboard

The keyboard is another way to shuttle and hunt through video—there are keyboard equivalents for almost all the on-screen controls. It utilizes different skills and provides slightly different control from the mouse. For instance, there is no "drag." You can hop around from control to control, but your hands are relatively fixed. Most keyboard controls for beginners are optimal for one hand, probably your right. When you get good and learn more keyboard functions, you'll find you can edit with two hands, just as if you're typing. This book will not go into that. I suggest not trying to learn all the keyboard functions right away; add shortcuts only as your confidence grows.

Space Bar

The best thing about the keyboard is that big ol' space bar: it functions as Play/Stop. It takes up about eight times the space of any of the other keys, so you know it's got to be important.

With the same VidClip1 in the Viewer, make sure the Viewer is active and press the space bar to play and press it again to stop.

Now let's learn how to move faster and back up, as you did with the shuttle knob.

J, K, L

Line up the J, K, and L keys under the first three fingers of your right hand, and you use them like this.

J = Play backward

K = Stop

L = Play forward

By pressing a kind of pattern, L ... K ... J ... K ... L you rock and roll over a given spot. You could skip the K—there's no need to stop between going forward and backward, but sometimes the point is about trying to stop on a frame to look at it, so you roll back, stop, look at it, roll forward a bit, stop, look again, and so on. But yes, you could just go back and forth, back and forth (L-J, L-J).

These are nice controls for rockin' and rollin'. If you want to move faster than playspeed, you simply press the J or L again and get *more* speed: pressed once you go at playspeed, twice is 2X speed, three times is 4X, and four times is 8X.

I sometimes use these keys for their multi-hit speed shuttling, but if it feels like what I'm looking for isn't nearby, I tend to grab hold of the mouse and try to go faster, probably using the scrubber bar.

If you want to get even fancier, you can use the K (stop) at the *same time* as the J or L, to crawl in either direction. This requires holding one finger down while tapping or moving the adjacent finger. It can take a little more coordination for the novice. A nice feature of using the K with the J or L is that the audio pitch changes as you move. Again, there are times you want to hear unaffected audio, and there are times when a pitch change is nice.

Using J, K, L along with the space bar, you'll enjoy an entire range of fine controls.

Arrow Keys

Most keyboards also have arrow keys for navigation. The left and right arrows serve as *step* forward and backward: a single-frame movement. This is my favorite way to move frame by frame. I repeatedly press the arrow to move around when I am close to where I think I need to be and want to examine the frames more closely. Play-speeds, and even slow crawls, are just too fast sometimes. They actually slow me down because I have trouble hitting the right spot. If you hold the arrow key down, the video will start jogging in that direction, slowly. Again, an excellent way to move around.

Repeatedly hitting a key, like the one-frame step arrows, may not always be the most efficient way to look around, but it is remarkably simple. And as a side benefit, it makes editing feel a little bit like a videogame—think a Fire/Shoot button in Asteroids (if you're over 30) or Tomb Raider (if you're not).

Other dedicated keys can be used to pop from beginning to end of a clip, or between various marks that you can place within the clip—but let's skip placing marks for the moment and just work on keyboard target practice.

A Special Kind of Navigation

The up and down arrow keys perform a special kind of navigation in your material. They pop you either toward the head of your clip (up) or toward the tail (down), stopping only at special points of interest along the way. In the Viewer, the arrows stop at each mark (In or Out) on their way to the head or tail of the clip. In the Canvas, where there are usually many more intermediary marks and edits, they move you edit-by-edit in whichever direction you're going (yes, they also stop at In and Out marks). It's a terrific way to move quickly around in a sequence or clip.

The on-screen controllers for this function are these buttons located near the Play button in both the Canvas and Viewer.

These navigation tools are excellent for moving around in clips, but aren't ideal for finding frames within a shot, as you are at this point in your precision-control practice. We'll revisit these alternate forms of navigation later, when we get into editing.

Target Practice

1 Double-click the VidClip1 icon in the Browser again.

This opens the clip in the Viewer window. You are now looking at the first captured frame of this clip. You could just click on the Viewer itself, if you know the clip you want to play is there, but if you're ever confused, this is the surefire way to establish that you're looking at (and controlling) the clip you think you are.

2 Using the keyboard, try to stop on the flash frame again.

First use the space bar.

Next use the JKL buttons.

Finally, play around with these in combination with the arrow keys, if you have them.

Putting Them All Together

I edit primarily with one hand, my right hand (since I'm right handed). I mostly use a mouse (or trackball) to click on things on the screen, but I let go and switch to slamming the space bar or settling into the JKL or arrow keys to do more detailed selecting and marking. Ultimately, I go back to the mouse to make the edits and move the Timeline around.

You will find your own balance. Here's a chance to practice.

A Scavenger Hunt

Now we move on to VidClip2. It's been sitting in your Browser, hopefully abandoned until now. Double-click it and begin to play it in the Viewer. Use your thumb on the space bar to start and stop it.

Marking In and Out

Playing around through your video, and having fine control of that motion, is important for the editor, but the all-important moment of editing is when you "tell" the computer that you have found what you are looking for by *marking* a frame.

 An *In mark* says "this is the beginning."

 An *Out mark* says "this is the end."

> **VOCABULARY: Marking**
>
> *Marking* a frame means placing a special "mark" onto the clip at a specific point. The hole punch used to mark the clap at the beginning of a shot is one kind of filmmaker's mark. The most important kind for our purposes are the marks you make that tell FCP "this is where the shot I like begins" and its sibling "this is where the shot I like ends."

When you edit, you are marking the in and out of a segment of a clip, and moving just that segment into your sequence.

 This button marks an In.

 This button marks an Out.

Marking In and Out is so critical that you should be equally adept at doing it with hands on the keyboard.

The I key marks In.

The O key marks Out.

Notice how conveniently close they are to the J, K, and L keys. (It's lucky that I and O are next to each other. It makes this all so much more logical.)

We aren't going to do any editing right now, but I want you to practice using the Mark In and Mark Out buttons to mark frames I have designated in VidClip2. Use mouse or keyboard or both to get to the desired frames and mark them. Most of what you do as an editor relates to your fluidity at performing this little activity.

Targets

As you play through this clip, you'll notice six kinds of flash frames. I'm using three punches: circle, square, and triangle. I have two sizes: large and small. And I have three lengths: one, two, and three frames. I've created nine "targets," which I have hidden within the 100 seconds of VidClip2. The background video (of my friend

Chris playing around in his yard) is designed to be somewhat distracting, although I have not buried these targets as invisibly as I could have done. All are readily locatable.

When you double-click on VidClip2 in the Browser, the first frame will pop up in the Viewer:

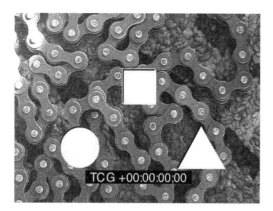

Here I have placed examples of the three shapes in their "small" size. You are looking for these flashes in the rest of the clip.

As you go through this obstacle course, take mental notes:

- How "long" does $1/30$th of a second feel versus $2/30$ths ($1/15$th) and $3/30$ths ($1/10$th)? Savor this sensation.

- How quick is your reaction time using different methods of stopping the moving video? At playspeed, after a target first flashes how many frames are you from it when you stop?

- How good are you at noticing small targets versus large ones? Sometimes the thing you search for in your video is not a scene, but something within the scene: a hand opening or a ball touching the floor. These can be subtle.

- How distracting is the background "content?" As an editor, you have to be able to turn on and off your attachment to what is going on in the narrative of your project in order to find things you are looking for in the shots.

The Hunt Is On

Play through the video, and mark an In on the first frame of the two-frame small circle target.

Mark an Out on the one-frame small triangle.

Easy?

I want to point out something to you: the timecode window. Not the big one I burned into the picture (called a "burn-in window"—embedded permanently in the picture itself), but the small window at the top

left of both the Viewer and the Canvas. It's called the *Timecode Duration* window, and it provides a handy little bit of information: the elapsed time between the In mark and the Out mark.

If you marked the In and Out points correctly on the first two targets, your duration timecode counter should say:

00:00:04;25

Got it? You should be getting the feel for shuttling around, stopping, and moving to a specific frame. You need to be very comfortable with this. You will do it all the time. More than any other single thing in editing.

This is probably a good time to look down at the bottom of the Viewer. Look at the scrubber bar. As we discussed earlier, the bar represents the entire duration of

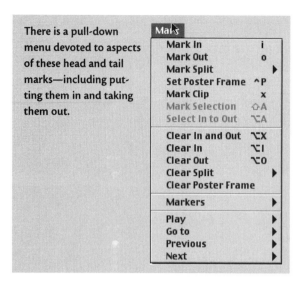

There is a pull-down menu devoted to aspects of these head and tail marks—including putting them in and taking them out.

Marks

Mark In	i
Mark Out	o
Mark Split	▶
Set Poster Frame	^P
Mark Clip	x
Mark Selection	⇧A
Select In to Out	⌥A
Clear In and Out	⌥X
Clear In	⌥I
Clear Out	⌥O
Clear Split	▶
Clear Poster Frame	
Markers	▶
Play	▶
Go to	▶
Previous	▶
Next	▶

this 100-second video. You should clearly see two marks now within this bar, near the front. The first is the In mark you made at the circle target; the second is the Out mark you made at this triangle target. Keep an eye on the scrubber for the marks you make as you go along.

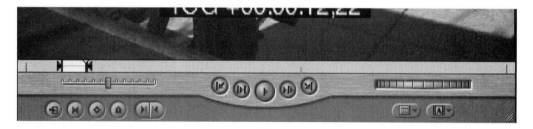

On the top right of the Viewer (and Canvas, too) is a second timecode window, called the Current Timecode display. This shows you the source timecode number of the clip in the Viewer; in the Canvas

it presents the master timecode number wherever the playhead is parked. Since my burn-in window began at 00:00:00;00, it turns out the number on the burn-in will pretty much match the small "live" number on the FCP interface (except for the 01 in the first position—but let's ignore the hours right now). Check to see that at the Out point the running time is 12 seconds, 22 frames. That's all you need to know at this point about the on-screen timecode windows.

To complete this scavenger hunt, I want you to fill in the blanks with the last four digits of timecode as they appear in the burn-in window at the bottom center of the screen.

1   The timecode for the large, one-frame circle: _____

Mark a new Out here. (Look at the scrubber bar. Also notice the Out mark on the top-right corner of the video. This is one of a handful of little marks called *overlays* that FCP superimposes on special frames for you.)

2   Find the one-frame small square; enter the timecode here: _____

Mark a new In here.

Notice that when an In point falls after an Out point, the Out point disappears (similarly, if an Out falls before an In). Also be aware that you are only allowed one In and one Out per clip. Thus every time you press In or Out, the location of this mark moves to the most recent spot. This can be useful.

While still on the small one-frame square, mark an Out. There are now both an In and an Out here. Note that the two marks appear simultaneously on the screen (as well as in the scrubber).

3   The duration between these marks: _____

When you are parked on a single frame, it can be both the beginning and the end of a shot, and the shot would therefore be one frame long.

Now go back toward the beginning of the video clip, back to the first target we found—to the first frame of the two-frame, small circle target. Mark a new In here.

Why am I asking you to return to the first target? Because you're learning one of the great advantages of using the scrubber bar to navigate here. You know sort of where you're looking, because we started at the scrubber a few moment ago when it was marked. So we're not randomly searching for it, but have a general idea. Clicking in the scrubber bar pops you to that location without forcing you to scroll through video. Then, once you're close, it's easier to scroll around looking for the frame you want.

At any rate, if you did it right, the duration should read 36;14.

Now go ahead and find (and write down the timecode for) the rest of these marks, listed here in no particular order:

4   The large one-frame square: _____

5   The large one-frame triangle: _____

6   The last frame of the small three-frame square: _____

7   The middle frame of the small three-frame triangle: _____

8   The small one-frame circle: _____

(Answers appear in the back of the book.)

Now that you've mastered moving your video around, been up and down the interface, and shuttled in every direction at every speed, with fine control, you are ready to cut something. As you edit more, you will be rehearsing without even trying the skills we have focused on in this chapter.

CHAPTER 2 Basic Editing

When you sit down and look at any editing system, you're assailed by buttons and windows and images and doohickies...so of course it seems complicated. In truth, people have been editing film using little more than a razor blade and a roll of tape for nearly a hundred years. Editing is really not that hard.

Most of the complexity in Final Cut Pro comes from the fact that there are almost always two and often three or four ways to accomplish every kind of editing function. This is why the interface for editing can appear complicated when it's really not that bad. To see how simple editing can be, we're going to ignore many features of FCP. It's not that they're unnecessary, it's just that many perform functions that either don't come up that often or are particularly advanced.

To make it simple, we'll work tutorial-style with the material from the DVD rather than focus on particular FCP functions. We'll edit a very basic scene together, exploring only the tools necessary to do the trick, and only as they become required. Your skills will build on each other and grow in power as they accumulate.

The Scene

```
LIVINGROOM -- DAY

CHRIS is sitting in a comfy overstuffed chair, reading a
magazine.  KIRSTEN enters.  She holds something in her hands,
but we can't see it at this point.

She stands before CHRIS, miffed perhaps, waiting for him to
take notice of her.  In a moment, he does.
                         KIRSTEN
                Do you love me?

CHRIS looks up, perplexed by the question.  He is certain in
his response.
                         CHRIS
                Yes.

KIRSTEN eyes him incredulously.

                         KIRSTEN
                I found these next to your bed.  You
                could have told me about this... I
                don't understand why you felt you
                had to hide this stuff... Chris?
                You're supposed to be able to talk
                to me...

While she rants, she holds something we still can't see;
CHRIS slowly looks down to see what it is she has.  His face
drops with his recognition of what she has found.  His jaw
opens, grasping helplessly for some kind of explanation.

                ...So I'll ask you again... do you
                love me.
                         CHRIS
                     (less sure this time,
                      maybe convincing
                      himself)
                Yes... yes...
                         KIRSTEN
                More than chocolate?

He is unable to answer... he looks from her face to the bag.
And back... silent... apologetic.  She is incensed.  Without
warning she throws the bag at him and storms out of the room.

CHRIS opens the bag to reveal a pile of imported dark
chocolate bars.

CUT TO BLACK

There is the sound of a candybar wrapper being torn open...
the sound of munching...
```

Here's our script (it's also in the Extras folder on your DVD, in an Adobe Acrobat file called chocoluv.pdf).

I shot this scene in my living room with a couple friends. It's not part of a real movie and these aren't actors. I used a clapboard, sometimes called a *slate*, at the beginning of most shots so you'd clearly see where each begins and ends, and so you'd have a basic label for each. There's a punch on the first frame of each shot (not at the clap) to help delineate the clips.

Videographers and professionals spend an appropriately lengthy part of their time organizing these distinct slated shots. Organization is fundamental in complex productions, and lack of organizational discipline will make even simple projects impossible to bring off. We will look at how scripts, material, and editing systems can be organized together, but we'll save that for later. For now, just familiarize yourself with the script and shots we'll be using to practice editing in the next three chapters.

Shot Vocabulary Cheat Sheet

TYPES OF SHOTS

Close Up (CU)
Head alone
A shot of one person is called a "single"

Medium Shot (MS)
Head to waist
A shot of two people is also called a "2-shot" (2/s)

Wide Shot (WS)
Head to toe
This one is particularly far away—
referred to as an "Extreme Wide Shot" or EWS.

SPECIAL SHOT RELATIONSHIPS

shot ⟶ reverse shot

shot ⟶ insert shot

shot ⟶ point of view (POV)

shot ⟶ establishing shot (ES)

I filmed the scene in a traditional way: close, medium, and wide shots on the man (Chris), close and medium on the woman (Kirsten), and then a couple close-up detail shots for use as *cut-aways*.

Chocoluv Tutorial

Among the tutorial files you copied onto your hard disk in Chapter 1, I included one project called "Chocoluv Tutorial" into which I placed the video clips, already broken down into individual takes and logged. Although I capture video as a single long clip (to save the time of logging) for most personal projects, professionals break up source material into clips like this for each distinct take.

Before editing, it's a good idea to watch your dailies (script in hand, in case you want to make notes), and familiarize yourself with the footage. In this project I have created a sequence for you, labeled "Dailies Reel," where all these distinct shots are reassembled into a single 11-minute "roll"—pretty much the way they were on the tape before I captured them into the computer.

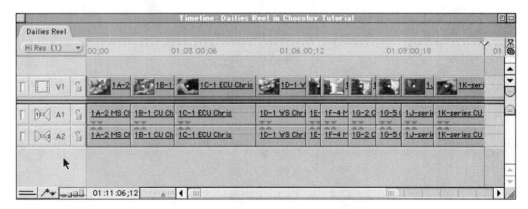

Reviewing Your Coverage

When you open this project (double-click the project icon), it will look mostly empty, but notice the clips I placed here for you in the Browser. Let's look at our coverage.

Here are single frames illustrating each camera shot (set-up), with basic descriptions:

Scene 1A, Take 2
MED Chris

Scene 1B, Take 1
CU Chris

Scene 1C, Take 1
ECU Chris

Scene 1D, Take 1
WS Chris

Scene 1E, Take 1
ECU Chris Hands

Scene 1F, Take 4
MS Kirsten

Scene 1G, Takes 2 and 5
CU Kirsten

Scene 1J, series of shots
CU Bag (Kirsten)

Scene 1K, series of shots
CU Bag (Chris)

Double-click the Dailies Reel in the Browser to move it into the Timeline and Canvas. Play this sequence and take notes on your script. A script is more than lines of dialog. For the editor, it's an organizational outline. The notes you take about the coverage, when placed on the script, form the basis

for your work; they will essentially dictate how you approach the material. My script notes about what was shot look like this:

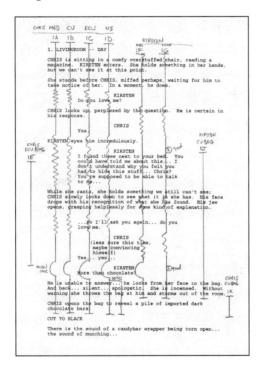

Here's a standard method of annotating a script (performed by the "script supervisor," who records notes and continuity issues). A solid line means the character is speaking on camera, a wavy line means they're not. At a glance, an editor can see which set-ups (1A, 1B, and so on) cover which parts of the scene. This is sometimes called a "lined script."

When you launch FCP for the first time it opens an unnamed project, with no clips yet captured, and one default sequence (called "Sequence 1") already in the Browser and Timeline, ready for you to add things to it. This is convenient. Even though I have created this project for you, and placed

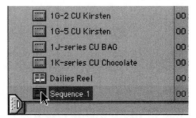

some clips in the Browser, I have left the empty Sequence 1 here for you to open.

Double-click Sequence 1 in the Browser. Notice it opens a clean, empty Timeline. The Canvas, too, will be empty.

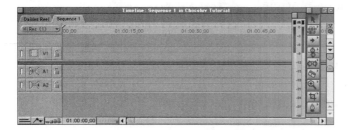

Look for Tabs

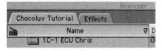

You'll now notice two tabs above the Timeline, one labeled "Dailies Reel" and the other "Sequence 1."

Look around the display for other tabs; every window has them, and they do slightly different things wherever they're used.

Tabs in the Browser let you access different projects that are open at the same time. Note: There is always one tab for your Effects toolset, but I'd like you to ignore it until Chapter 5.

Tabs in the Viewer let you view different "slices" through a clip. For now we only want to look at the *video* slice—the Viewer display usually shows the picture of the selected source clip; but there is an *audio* slice that shows waveforms of the stereo sound tracks; a *filter* slice that outlines the filters you've applied to this video; and a *motion* slice for the motion effects you've applied.

Tabs in the Timeline bring up different sequences that are open at the same time. These can even be sequences from different projects.

Tabs in the Canvas show the same sequences that have tabs in the Timeline. As in the Timeline, you can see any sequences that are presently open, even if you aren't watching them.

Editing Your First Shots

Let's make our first edit. Glancing at the script, you'll see that the scene begins with Kirsten asking Chris the question "Do you love me?" You can see from my "lined" script that we have some options for this first

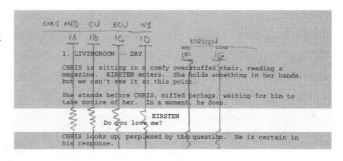

line of dialog. There are two shots (but three takes) of Kirsten saying this line: two in close and one in medium. For the moment, we're not concentrating on the quality of her "performance"; we just want to get the line delivered on camera.

1   Select the clip labeled 1F-4 in the Browser, and double-click it to open it in the Viewer.

2   Play the clip, using the space bar or other controls you learned in Chapter 1. (If you have any trouble, go back to Chapter 1 and review the "Playtime" section.)

3   Watch the shot until she utters her first word, then back up a little, and mark an In. When you press Play again, there should be a moment of silence (called a *beat*) before she starts talking.

4   When she finishes her line, press Stop and mark an Out. Make sure you aren't hearing any other audio at the point you choose to mark an In or an Out. (Finding these In and Out points involves exactly the kind of precision shuttling with the jogwheel, JKL keys, or frame-by-frame stepping that we covered in the last chapter.) Your Viewer should look approximately like this:

Insert

Click and hold on a clip in the Viewer and you can drag it around. Drag it onto the Canvas. It looks like you're dragging a little icon of the shot as you move, and when you reach the window, a translucent menu (called the Canvas Edit Overlay) pops up with a handful of choices for "how" you want to put this shot into the edited sequence. Drag the clip to Insert and drop it.

The Insert button is large and pretty easy to hit. When you let go, you'll notice the shot appears full-frame in the Canvas and also below in the Timeline.

Congrats: You're editing.

Before we move on, let's look around the screen:

OUT FRAME ICON

SEQUENCE RUNNING TIME (AT THE PLAYHEAD)

MARKED CLIP DURATION

ORIGINAL CLIP

OUR CLIP

THE TIMELINE

STEREO AUDIO TRACKS (A1 AND A2)

ONE VIDEO TRACK (V1)

Compare the original clip in the Viewer with the clip you just inserted into the Timeline, and you'll see that they currently have the same duration (look in the Marked Duration timecode window, top left).

The timecode windows at the top right of the Viewer and Canvas are the Current Timecode displays. The one in the Viewer provides you with the timecode of the source material. The one in the Canvas provides you with the elapsed time from the start of the sequence (the master timecode). Since we have only one shot in our sequence so far, the running time for the sequence is also (mostly) the same as the duration of the clip. (A little later in this chapter I'll explain why some timecodes begin with 01 instead of 00; focus on the last four digits right now.) You can also see in the Timeline that the video track and stereo audio tracks are actually three separate items, even though they move as one. For now, at least.

Feeling OK?

To make sure you are comfortable with your screen, click the tab labeled "Dailies Reel" (in either the Canvas or the Timeline, it doesn't matter).

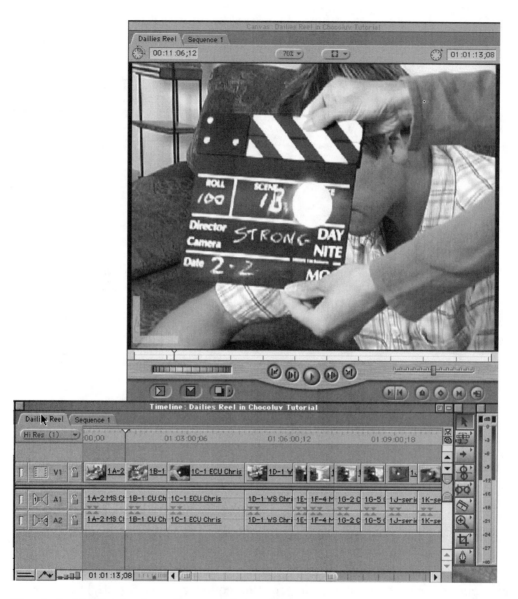

Here's the Dailies Reel just how you left it. We don't need it, so go back to the Sequence 1 tab. You could go back and forth all day just like this.

Just for fun, *without watching the material you edited in Sequence 1*, let's go get another shot to add onto the end of this one. (If you went ahead and watched, make sure you're now parked at the end of the first, and only, shot. If you aren't, the next few moments may get confusing.)

1 Go to the Browser and double-click shot 1A-2, the medium shot of Chris; now scroll into it until you hear Kirsten's line finish and before Chris responds.

2 Mark an In here, but do *not* mark an Out:

When you don't mark an In or an Out, FCP makes some assumptions about what you're doing. If you don't mark an Out, FCP assumes the end of the clip is the Out, and if you don't mark an In, it assumes the beginning of the clip is the In. Thus (until you are quite advanced), every clip always has two and only two marks in it. You can move them around, but there are always two—no more, no less.

3 As before, drag this shot over to the Canvas and drop it on the Insert button.

After you let go, what has changed? You'll see a large clip added to the Timeline, that appears to be substantially longer than the first shot, and there is the playhead parked at the end. FCP cues up the last frame of the shot you just edited, which in this case is the tail of 1A-2 and shows it to you in the Canvas

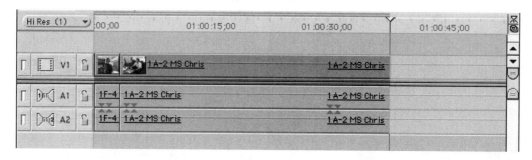

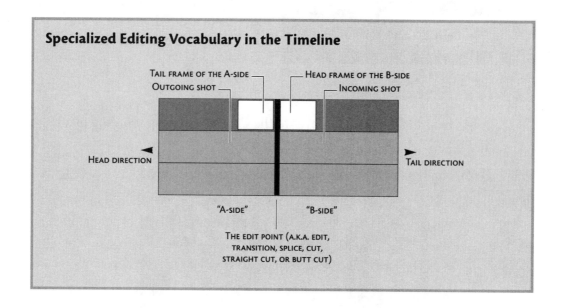

The Insert Concept

What you have been doing is *inserting*. In editing, "inserting" as a general concept is taking source material and adding it to the edited sequence. In practical FCP terms, it means taking material from the Viewer and moving it into the Canvas. This may not seem that different from the dictionary definition of the word *insert*, but it's special, because it's not enough simply to insert source material into the master, an editor needs to know *how* it should be inserted; the function FCP calls Insert is more generally described as a "ripple insert." Which brings us to the concept of "rippling."

VOCABULARY: **Insert**

The word *insert* is used in special ways throughout the filmmaking process, which (like *master*) sometimes can be a little confusing.

1   NOUN A camera shot with a special relationship to the master shot. An insert is a close, detail view of some object that was also visible in the wider master shot. Similar to a "cut-away" an insert is a special case because it is specifically about providing more info on something the audience has already seen.

2   VERB To take a source material and place it into the edited sequence. Not all source material is "clips"; you can also insert other sequences.

3   NOUN Slang for any picture-only shot that is dropped over a region of the picture of a sync shot (picture and sound).

4   NOUN The general editing term for putting source shots in the master sequence, either with or without rippling.

5   NOUN The FCP term for a "rippling insert."

It would be correct (but ridiculous) to say: "I used the *insert* (FCP function) from the keyboard command to *insert* (put in) that *insert* (the slang) of the black-and-white *insert* (camera) shot."

You can play these shots a number of ways in the Timeline. I like simply to pop to the mark In and press Play:

  or up arrow and spacebar on the keyboard. You can drag the playhead to the beginning of the Timeline. You can press the up arrow on the keyboard twice (once gets you to the edit you just made, the second time takes you to the head of the sequence). There are no right or wrong ways to navigate and play.

The Ripple Concept

Everything that happens in editing—every manipulation you make to an edited sequence—can be characterized as one of two types: a manipulation that *ripples* and one that does not. So what is rippling?

Imagine you're stacking toy blocks. When you insert a block into the middle of the stack, every block above the insertion point will shove higher. When you pull a block out of the middle (if you're careful), all the blocks above it will drop down to fill the gap. The stack must move up or down every time you make a change to the blocks. This is rippling.

Turn the stack on its side (that is, line up the blocks on the floor), and you can now remove a block without moving the others. If you choose to close the gap, you're rippling the blocks. If you decide to leave the gap, you're not rippling them.

Similarly, as you make adjustments or add material to your edited shots, it seems natural for the shots to ripple around, sliding back and forth to make room for the changes, but keeping all the individual shots themselves unchanged and still connected. In fact, rippling is sometimes referred to as a "film-style" edit, because film is edited with changes that push and pull all the other shots around.

If you're trying to keep different tracks in sync with each other, a ripple in one track will invariably throw it out of sync with the others. This is why rippling is also sometimes considered dangerous (or advanced) and the icons for it in professional editing systems have historically been colored red. Final Cut Pro colors them yellow, reminding you that, while it could be dangerous, you will never accidentally erase something by inserting; proceed with caution.

The alternative to rippling is, of course, *not* rippling. In general (but not always), FCP refers to this as *rolling*. Whatever the function is called (not-rippling, rolling, overwriting), it means that whatever modification you perform, the overall length of the edited sequence will not change.

So if you add two seconds to something in the Timeline, two seconds are automatically removed from the material already in the Timeline. A zero-sum game, as they say. When you perform operations that don't ripple, you can never accidentally throw your tracks out of sync from each other, even if you're only making changes to one track. In that sense, a non-ripple modification is "safe." However, because you might inadvertently remove material, there is a more serious chance of ruining something in your sequence. For this reason, not-ripping is considered more dangerous than rippling, and thus is color-coded in red.

Let's Do Two More Inserts

First, let's put a shot ahead of the first shot in the sequence. Let's see Chris as Kirsten enters.

1 Open clip 1A-2 into the Viewer again. Notice that the part we used is still marked with an In point (we never marked an Out).

2 Drag the playhead across the scrubber to move ahead of the In point, and find Chris sipping his coffee, before Kirsten enters.

3 Mark a new In point, and you'll see the old one disappear and move to your new playhead location.

We're also going to find an Out point—somewhere before anyone talks. This little bit of video, before the action starts, will work to establish this scene.

1 In the Viewer, scrub around to find the frame where you want this shot to end.

2 Mark an Out.

We've now marked clip 1-A2 with two points—an In and an Out point. Now we need to tell FCP where we want to put it. FCP inserts wherever the playhead is parked. Therefore, we want to move the playhead to the beginning of the sequence.

It may be a little hard to see in the Timeline, but the Canvas should be cued up to the first frame. How do you know it's the first ("head") frame? FCP has a different icon it superimposes on the Canvas images to indicate head and tail frames of shots as edited. These right-angle icons in the Canvas indicate your playhead is parked on a head or tail frame of a clip in the Timeline. Like I said, the Timeline and the Canvas go together.

With everything lined up properly, drag clip 1-A2 from the Viewer to the Canvas, and insert it right here. This is what should happen:

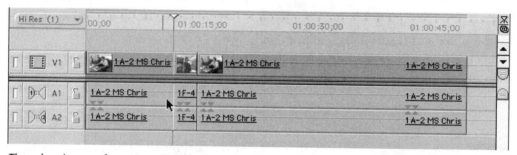

Three shots in a row, from 1A to 1F and back to 1A.

Notice that when you inserted a shot ahead of the other two, it shoved those two down to run a little later. We *rippled* them. This is a ripple insert. (Final Cut Pro calls this simply an "Insert." But you should understand the distinction.)

Just to drive this point home, let's do one more.

Play the sequence from the beginning one more time and be ready to hit the Stop button (any Stop button). Play through the three shots and stop just after Chris finishes his line with the word *no*. He's kind of smirking in this take anyway, so see if you can get the part of his performance where he's credible. It's short.

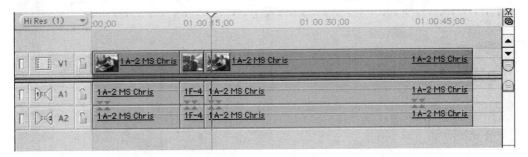

Now, leave the Timeline and Canvas for a moment. You've found the natural end of Chris's shot. It's time to move back to the source material and find Kirsten's reaction.

Let's start with 1F-4 again. We used it before. Maybe we'll use some more.

Double-click 1F-4 in the Browser and it will appear on the Viewer. Notice it's right where you left it. Press Play and see what Kirsten does next.

She says her line of dialog, of course. Let's see what other coverage we have for this line. Maybe there is a particularly good delivery of this line in another take. Double-click 1G-2 in the Browser.

Since we've never used this clip before, you'll see it cue up to the head frame when it shows up in the Viewer (and there are no marks in the scrubber). Notice the FCP screen icon superimposed over our images—that is, the sprocket holes on the left side of the frame (FYI: this is the third FCP icon we've seen thus far: first were the In/Out marks; second the head/tail of a shot in a sequence). The sprocket holes indicate that the image you are seeing is the first of a clip. You'll see the same icon on the right of the image when it's the last of a clip.

Play through this shot and mark an In and Out around Kirsten's response. Do the same thing with 1G-5. You can now directly compare her delivery of this line in the two takes.

You've now seen all the coverage you have of Kirsten; insert the take you like. I used 1G-5.

Even though the playhead wasn't parked between two shots, when we indicated we wanted to insert (and ripple) this new shot, FCP ripped open the sequence right where we were parked and dropped it in. Then it shoved the rest of 1A-2 down. Play your sequence now, and you'll see what I mean.

So there's your cut so far, and then it trails off into 1A-2 material you don't want. It's time to move on from inserting to fix-

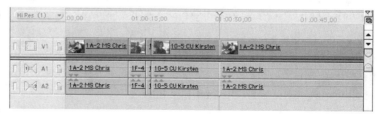

ing. But before we start fixing what we've got, let's take a break and get a closer look at the graphical display of our edits: the Timeline.

Some Timeline Features

The Timeline is its own little landscape in FCP. Because it graphically represents your cut as if you were connecting *real* objects, you should continue to get familiar with its odd nuances.

Reminder: The up and down arrow keys in the Viewer move you from the head to the tail of a clip. In the Timeline, these arrows pop you headward or tailward through your sequence, one edit at a time.

Scale

The Timeline has a yardstick across the top, which represents the scale of time against which the clips are measured. Increasing the window width will, of course, show more of your sequence, but you can also accomplish this by changing the scale. As your sequences grow in length, you may want to see more at a time for editing reasons (say you want to move an entire scene or you want to see how long one area is, compared to another). There are also more practical, functional reasons (say your shots are hard to grab, see, or work with).

FCP Time

Time is written in FCP in the traditional timecode format: hours, minutes, seconds, and frames, each separated by a colon (00:00:00:00). You'll see this notation in all the timecode and duration windows scattered across the interface. In many cases, and in particular with the Timeline, you'll see that time does not start at 0, but instead at 1 hour. This is a holdover from professional video days. Tapes traditionally start at 1 hour straight up (01:00:00:00) and so do the sequences in FCP. For more on timecode, see Chapter 5.

There are lots of ways to adjust the scale and zoom in on the Timeline. Let's look at two good ways now.

1 The Zoom control is nestled in the lower frame of the Timeline window:

As you move the small center pointer left and right over the scale, you'll see the Timeline squeeze or stretch correspondingly. When the little scale lines draw closer together, so will the graphic representation of your cuts. Similarly, when the scale lines move wider apart, the Timeline will also expand, like an accordion, to display the shots larger, with more space between cuts.

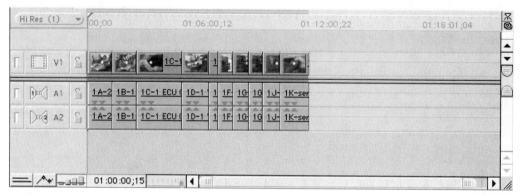

Notice the scale across the top. Here the "Dailies Reel" has been squished to fit—there's almost 12 minutes of video represented.

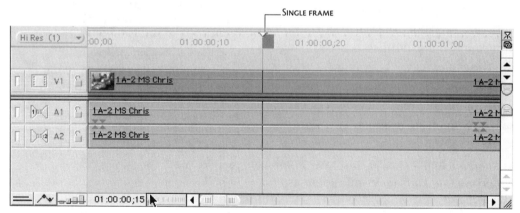

When it's zoomed in tight, the Timeline only represents about a second of video. It's so close, in fact, that you can see the way FCP places the playhead at a *single* frame and highlights it in the Timeline.

2 You can also zoom using the magnifying glass from the toolbox. With this tool, you can pinpoint a spot you want to see in detail, and click repeatedly to zoom in to the scale that works for you. (Option-click to zoom out.)

Adjusting Your Shots

Now that you've made some edits, let's change them a little. There are two primary ways to fix things already cut into your sequence. The first is by trimming the transitions that are there, and the second is by deleting material from anywhere in the sequence.

The Trim Concept

Trimming means changing the transition (called the *edit point* in FCP) where two shots are joined. It can mean adding or subtracting frames—to either side of the selected transition. But trimming is *always* about the two shots that are there now, in the Timeline.

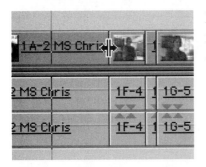

Let's take a close look at a trim. Move your cursor in the Timeline over any transition. The cursor changes.

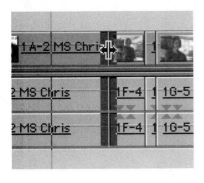

If you click on this transition once, you'll highlight this particular splice point. If you look closely at this dark gray highlight, it's actually highlighting a little on the tail of one shot and more on the head of the other. It's a thick bar. Keep this in mind as we get into trims.

Double-clicking will break the transition open into a special trim window (called the Trim Edit window) that goes on top of the Viewer and Canvas. It's not the same as the Viewer and Canvas, although it does look very similar:

For any trim, you will begin at the point where the tail of the outgoing shot is attached to the head of the incoming shot. This is known as the "edit" or "splice" or "splice point," but I also call it the "transition."

Imagine a piece of tape is holding these two shots together. A trim always takes place at the tape. Double-clicking on the transition itself "rips the tape off" and displays both the outgoing and incoming frames *at the same time*. Now you can decide if you want to adjust one or both sides of the splice.

> Editing software gives the impression that an edit is simply the point where one frame is taped to another frame. This trim window accentuates this notion because it shows you the two frames adjacent to the edit point. What you'll come to realize is that an edit isn't so much between two *frames* as between two *shots*. If you only look at the two frames at the edit point, you may never learn the art of playing with the way the shots move together and into each other.

Ripple Trim

With a trim, it's important to decide whether you want to change both sides of the transition together or individually. Much of the time you will want to make discrete decisions for each of the outgoing and incoming shots. You do this with the function called "Ripple Trim" in FCP.

As with any tool that ripples, a ripple trim will likely change the overall length of your edited sequence. To perform a ripple trim you must always choose one of the two shots that you wish to adjust. You adjust only one shot at a time, but you can still make independent modifications to both.

Let's do it in the trim window:

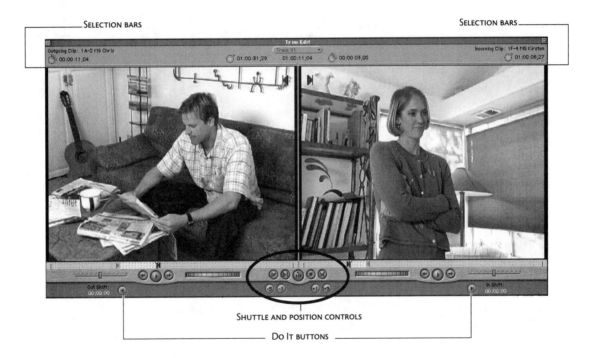

Here's where we left our stars. If you want to see how this transition looks, press the special Play Around Edit Loop button.

Let me point out a few elements of this window:

The Selection bars along the top are mission critical. You can't tell from this black-and-white photo, but they are bright green, and they indicate that both frames are currently locked together so that when you change one, you'll change the other. This won't work if you just want to adjust one side. Both sides are green because when you selected and double-clicked the transition in the Timeline, both sides were highlighted (remember?).

The Mark In and Mark Out buttons in the trim window are your "Do It" buttons. They allow you to move the Out or In point to a new location before reattaching these shots. They are no different from the Mark Out and Mark In buttons on your keyboard.

REMINDER: You can move around in the two shots with the shuttle controls all you want, but you won't be adjusting anything until you re-mark an In or Out. A common beginner's problem is forgetting to re-mark after playing the shots in the trim.

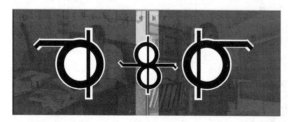

Try this: Move the cursor back and forth across the two frames in the trim window and notice how it changes into one of two icons. When the cursor is on the left side of the edit point, it's a left-handed Ripple Trim icon; on the right, it's right-handed. (When it's over the middle, it's a different trim icon—but we'll get to that.)

When you click one shot or the other with the Ripple Trim icon, it means that you're going to alter only one shot at a time. Click a frame with this icon and notice what happens to the green bars above the window. Also notice what happens to the highlight in the Timeline. Everything shifts to only one side of the transition.

When the bar is over only one shot, you're changing only that shot.

1 Click the outgoing shot of Chris on the left. The green bar will now be over 1A-2 only.

2 Use the shuttle controls in the trim window to move this shot around. Just like in the Canvas or Viewer, you can play, shuttle, scrub, and use the JKL and others. (The forward and back arrows don't work to move one frame at a time in the Trim Edit window, so I use the jogwheel to microadjust things.)

3 Adjust the outgoing shot of Chris so it ends just as Kirsten is leaving frame but is still visible. Make sure you press the Mark Out button again after you change the scrubber position in this shot.

4 Now, still in trim mode, click on the other side of the transition, so that the green bar is over clip 1F-4. Do the same adjustment, but this time back Kirsten up so she is just entering frame on the left.

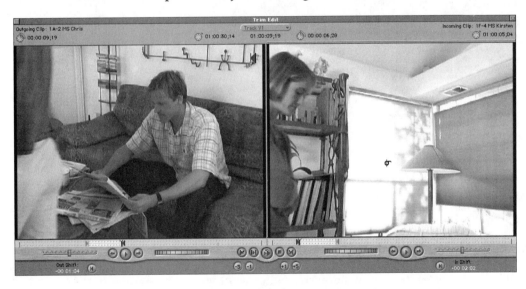

5 Now watch the transition by clicking the Play Around Edit Loop Button.

Ugh!

Well, you did the trim correctly, but the problem is one of editing *aesthetics*. While Kirsten is in about the same position in both shots, and she's exiting frame on one and entering frame on the other, her *screen direction* is wrong. She's moving right to left in the first shot, and left to right in the second, and the abrupt cut from one to the other doesn't work.

A better way to make this work is to let her leave frame totally in the first shot, and then let her enter the new shot. You're still in trim mode here, so repeat steps 3 and 4 to readjust the frames until the transition works better.

That's better. Anyway, that's the basis of ripple trimming.

When you're satisfied with your trim, all you need to do to get out of this window is click on the Timeline.

Rolling (Non-Rippling) Trim

Before you leave the trim window, though, I want you to try a non-rippling trim, called a Roll Trim in FCP. Let's move to the next transition, where Chris says "Yes."

When you are in a rolling trim mode, no matter how many frames you add or subtract to one side of a transition, the exact same number of frames are added or subtracted from the other side of the transition to keep the overall duration the same.

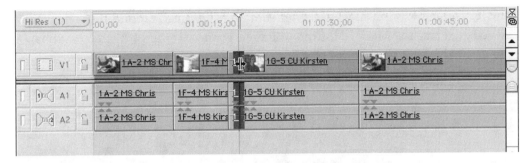

THIS IS THE ICON FOR A ROLLING TRIM.

Remember the green bar above the frames? In a rolling trim you want that bar over both shots. If you only see one green bar, move the cursor toward the middle of the window until it turns into the Roll icon, and click down.

Now, let's adjust Kirsten so we start her shot after her line "I found these next to the bed...." Press the Mark In button to indicate a new In point. Watch what happens to Chris's shot, and notice the Timeline.

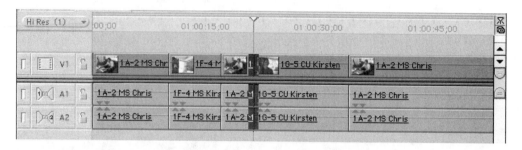

The transition moved, but none of the subsequent shots moved. It is as if the transition *slid* to the right. Also notice that the Out and the In shifted exactly the same amount (+2:25).

Play the cut. Personally, I don't think this works. Even in scripted material, it's probably better to adjust each side of a transition specifically to the right spot, and not together in this way. What you'll discover if you play with this enough is that this scenario is not the best editing situation for using a rolling trim, and I don't recommend using it right now. Just undo the edit and go back to the way it was before we started this.

We'll come back to rolling trims when they make more sense.

The Delete Concept

While *trimming* certainly seems like it means the same thing as *deleting,* you have seen that it isn't. Trimming can mean adding *or* removing frames. Sometimes you just want to take a knife and cut out something you don't like. There's no more fundamental way to do this than to delete it. And just like inserting and trimming, each time you remove material from a sequence, FCP must be told whether the change ripples or doesn't ripple the following shots.

There are a few different ways to delete material from your sequence, but almost all center on the use of the Razor Blade tool.

Razor Blade Tool

We haven't spent too much time using the tools in the on-screen toolbox. If you look in there, you'll see a cursor arrow, some odd things we haven't discussed, a Trim tool (you should recognize the Ripple or Roll Trim icon wherever you see it), and then there's a razor blade. Remember how all editing was done for years with little more than a razor blade? Here's your razor blade.

When you click the Razor Blade tool, your cursor is now a razor blade, and any place in the Timeline you click, you cut the sequence right there. Cutting doesn't really do anything. You can cut it up into lots of bits, but you won't notice any change when you play through the chopped up region. Cutting, however, creates bits that can be easily moved or deleted.

Lift (Non-Ripple Delete)

Let's say you dislike the way this whole scene begins. It looks like Chris is watching TV or something before Kirsten enters the frame. You could trim the head of his shot, but you could also just play the sequence until you see where you think it should start.

Notice as you move the razor blade into the Timeline that it's popping from transition to transition. When you get near the playhead, it pops there, and small triangular icons appear. Great. This is called *snapping* and it gets you right to the spot where you want to cut this shot. Click right here.

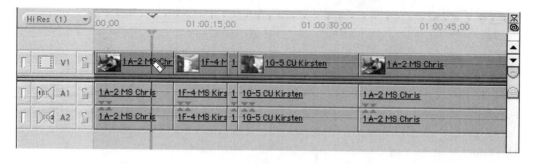

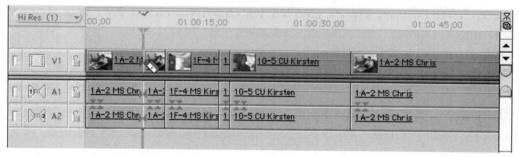

Snapping makes your cursor pop from key spot to key spot in your Timeline—edits, the playhead, some other marks. A number of tools in FCP have this snapping feature, an important one in FCP. So make a point to experiment with snapping as you grow more comfortable with the basic editing features. Snapping is on by default; to turn it off (or back on), click the snapping tool nestled in the frame of the Timeline window.

SNAPPING ON ———— 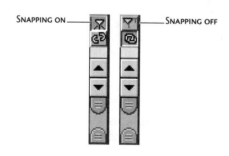 ———— SNAPPING OFF

Looking back at the Timeline, you'll see that the razor blade cut the first shot into two. We like the second part, but not the first. The slowest but simplest way to get rid of the first part is to take the arrow cursor, select this clip, and press Delete.

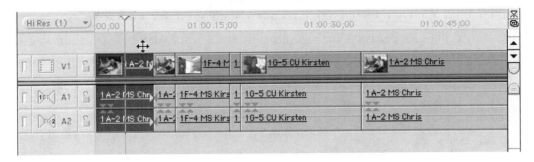

FCP doesn't call this "delete," however; it calls this "Lift."

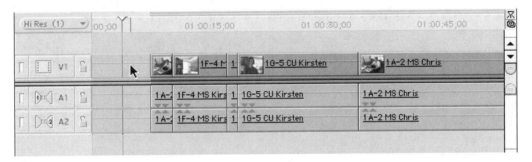

All you need to know is that *Lift* is another way of describing a non-rippling delete. You removed something from the Timeline, but instead of everything sliding down into place, filling the gap created, Lift just leaves things where they were. This is good to know, but it's less important for you now than deleting and rippling the shots down to fill the gap. So undo that Lift, and let's get to it.

Ripple Delete

Ripple delete is a powerful function. It can be faster than the trim mode, but more importantly, it can be the more efficient way to tighten shots as you work.

The only difference between performing a lift and a ripple delete is the Shift key—press Shift-Delete to ripple. This is not the only way to ripple delete, but it's how we'll do it here.

1 Select the first part of the shot (the part we don't like).

2 Hold down the Shift key and press Delete. The shot disappears and the other shots slide down neatly.

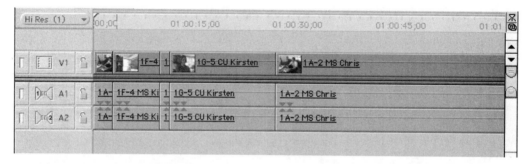

Still feeling OK? It may be dawning upon you that the handful of functions you now know are both fundamental and enormously powerful. If you're flummoxed by any of these basic concepts, this is the time to go back and work through the tutorial more slowly, making sure you're comfortable with the language and concepts. We're in no rush.

Saving Multiple Versions

Before we leave this chapter, I want to show you one more thing.

All the work we have been doing has been in Sequence 1. Go back to the Browser and locate this sequence.

1   In the Browser, click once on the name of the sequence. The sequence will be highlighted.

2   Click once more on the highlighted name, and it changes color. You can now change the name.

3   Type a new name for Sequence 1— I suggest "First Cut."

Regardless of what you may think of your "First Cut," it is good organization and a safe working habit to make copies of your work periodically. Not just backups of data, but new sequences that let you keep old versions around in case you need them.

To make a copy of your sequence,

1   Highlight it in the Browser.

2   Select Edit > Duplicate. This will place a copy in your Browser, conveniently named "First Cut Copy."

3   Change the name of one of these to something else—perhaps "Second Cut."

You now have two identical sequences with different names. Going forward we will work on Second Cut. Double-click Second Cut in the Browser (notice it opens in the Timeline and Canvas, and also notice all the tabs.)

Review of FCP Editing Tools

The cutting we have been doing in this chapter has been in both picture and sound together. These are known as *straight cuts,* because they all line up neatly in the Timeline across all tracks as you move through a sequence.

Although straight cuts are simple to do, they're still important. The first time I move through video material making edits, I do so with straight cuts (knowing I will be augmenting them later). I make my edits where there are pauses in dialog. This way, I control the breaths between those lines, which goes very far toward setting the tone and emotion of a scene. (I almost never cut between words.)

This first pass is about building the timing and rhythm of the dialog, and paying less attention to the picture. It's not that you won't change the timings later, but it's always easier to make changes to a scene with straight cuts than a scene complicated with lots of split tracks.

It is through control and use of this timing that good editors start to rise above the pack. By making the moments between lines of dialog short and fast, an editor can make a scene frantic or hostile or perhaps give the impression that characters are flirting; long pauses often make characters seem more pensive, serious, and emotional. Lots of things are going on in a movie when words are not being spoken.

The tools we have used in this chapter are sufficient to do many important things. With Rippling and Non-Rippling added to the basic editing functions of Inserting, Trimming, and Deleting, you can see the breadth of editing you can accomplish.

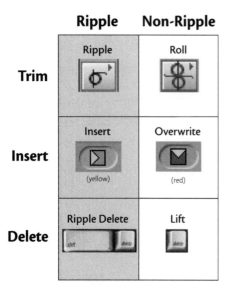

	Ripple	Non-Ripple
Trim	Ripple	Roll
Insert	Insert (yellow)	Overwrite (red)
Delete	Ripple Delete	Lift

Now is a good time to practice the skills we've just learned. Delete shots you don't like, go through the source material and cut together better performances of each line of the script, and see if you can cut the entire scene using insert, trim, and delete.

No doubt there will be things you want to do that you won't be able to accomplish with the tools we've discussed. Don't do them. Just get a feeling for what you *can* do with these features and without messing with audio tracks. Also, make sure you limit yourself to using straight cuts before you attempt the significantly more complex variations in the next chapter.

When you're done cutting the scene, compare your edits to mine. My edit is in the tutorial folder, labeled "Rubin Cuts." You can open this project without closing yours, using the project tabs in the Browser to move between them. Rubin Cuts contains a handful of sequences. My straight-cut version of this scene is called "Rubin's Cut 1"; we'll be using it as the starting place for the next chapter.

CHAPTER 3

Less Basic Editing

Everything we did in the last chapter, we did with straight cuts, that is, cuts with picture and sound held intractably in each other's arms. But what you will come to see is that one of the ways you hide edits in picture (and that is partly what editing is about) is by *burying* them in sound. Until you can split picture away from sound ("split the tracks") and manipulate each, individually as well as together, you will always be somewhat handicapped in your ability to edit.

I really had trouble cutting the Kirsten-and-Chris scene using only straight cuts. Often I wanted the video but not the sound, or I wanted to use Kirsten's off-camera line but to see Chris's face. Don't kid yourself, it can sometimes be harder to edit things when you can't split the tracks.

There are dangers with splitting tracks. Principal among these is "going out of sync." When picture and sound tracks slip apart from each other—even a single frame—managing them gets difficult, even if it isn't obvious there is a sync problem. When they go more than five frames out of sync, it becomes more and more visually irritating; in rare situations an audience has been known to lynch the projectionist.

Much of what we do in this chapter is about splitting tracks, but in such a way as to keep picture and sound from ever moving out of sync in the first place.

Track Controls

Here's your timeline at this point in the edit:

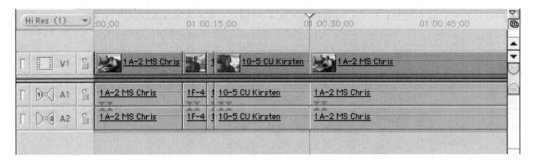

The timeline comprises three tracks running together, locked in sync: one of picture and two of sound (the left and right channels of stereo audio). They may seem like one immutable whole, but they are three tracks. We are going to start to treat them as such. (Actually, we'll still manage the two soundtracks together more like one. But that's a minor detail.)

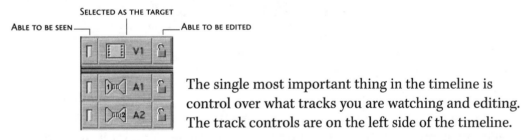

The single most important thing in the timeline is control over what tracks you are watching and editing. The track controls are on the left side of the timeline.

The columns here determine the state of the track—any one of three possible states. (In each of the following examples, I have modified the A1 track alone, so you can differentiate it from the other two.) In order of importance to us right now, they are...

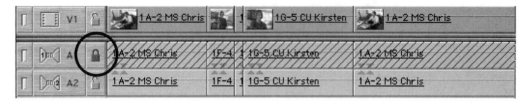

Able to be edited: The **lock/unlock state** simply locks down a track, so you can see (or hear) its contents, but you can't change it in any way. Until you are more advanced, this is the only track control I think you should mess with.

Able to be seen: The **green light on/off** means you are previewing in the Canvas the contents of this track. I rarely alter this.

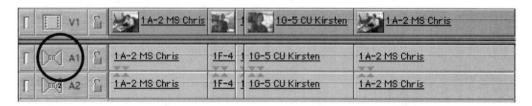

Targeted: This track has been selected as the target for a particular modification. Source material, by definition, is at most one picture and two sound tracks. So whenever you make an edit, FCP will want to know where you want it to put these three tracks. For us, working in picture and stereo audio, there's never a question that picture goes in the picture track, and so on. With advanced editing (which we'll do in Chapter 4), you will have multiple picture and sound tracks and it becomes important to specify the target track where you are putting a particular bit of source material. But not now.

If you look closely at the frame of the Timeline window, you'll see an array of embedded buttons and tools. They're interesting, and some are important, but none compare to the importance of the track controls—which of course is why they are big.

Tracks in FCP are virtually the same thing as *layers* in any graphics application. Track controls of this sort, then, are pretty much standard features of graphics applications and may be familiar. Though they're sometimes called different things, in general you always have at least the above three options for any layer.

Here are some track controls in Adobe Photoshop:

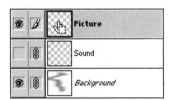

and here they are in Macromedia Freehand:

Notice that the green light in FCP is akin to the eyeballs (signaling whether or not you see the layer); and FCP's locks translate into locks or chains (signaling whether you can edit it). But they all amount to the same thing.

Locking vs. Linking

When you select a shot, you may notice that FCP is smart enough to select the *whole* shot—picture and sound tracks together. It does this because the separate tracks are *linked* together. Because they are linked, you can't select just one track, you can't change just one track—which is great because much of the time, this is exactly what you want to do. It would be laborious if every time you wanted to delete a frame or trim a second, you had to do it three times, once in each track.

But if I really *do* want to do something to only one track, I must be able to select it individually, without selecting the others. Now, there are tools that allow me to *permanently* unlink a picture track from its sound, but what we want here is something more temporary—to make FCP behave as if the clip were unlinked, but without losing that important link relationship. To select one track of a clip and not others, we need to change the Link Selection mode.

The button for changing this linking/unlinking mode (called the Linking toggle button) is very small, and it's nestled in the frame of the Timeline window just below the snapping control:

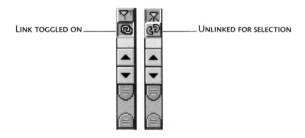

LINK TOGGLED ON ———— ———— UNLINKED FOR SELECTION

On the other hand, when I only want to change one track, it often makes more sense to lock the other tracks, and not change the link mode.

In our work it doesn't really matter which you choose—unlinking or unlocking. I will be using the track lock method in this chapter both because I really do use it, and because it's easier in the Timeline illustrations to see when I have a track locked (as opposed to having changed the Linked Selection mode).

The Overlap

People unconsciously expect edits to happen in places where one person stops talking and another starts. And by placing edits in these pauses, you make your edits that much more obvious to the viewer. Remember that one component of editing is hiding edits—not letting the audience realize they are watching something with cuts. Now, you might want jarring and you might not. But if you don't, you'll often want to move the picture cut *away* from the sound cut.

In other words: You want to see the person *not* talking for a little bit before or after he speaks.

You do this by sliding around the cut point between two pictures, while leaving the sound cut where it is: Slide it ahead of the sound cut, and you've created an L-cut (also called a *prelap*); slide it after the sound cut, and you've created a J-cut (*postlap*). I don't think the name (L or J, prelap or postlap) matters much. In either case, this is called a *split edit* or *overlap,* and it's done with a rolling (non-rippling) trim of the picture track alone.

There are many reasons to create overlaps. In the first place, they make a video more sophisticated. They make edit transitions more subtle, and give the editor a greater opportunity to sculpt a video that presents aesthetic nuances in greater detail.

It's said that in movies, it is often more important to see the person being spoken *to* than the person speaking; that you can determine more about a person's character watching them react to something than watching them move their lips. Overlaps are not only a good way to hide edits and soften transitions, but they also let viewers see more character revealed.

There's a small downside to overlaps: They make re-editing a little more complicated. They take time, and time is one thing every editor must be careful not to squander. But in the end, overlaps are important tools for all but the least experienced of beginners, and becoming good at them is a worthy skill.

Rolling Edit (Non-Rippling Trim) in Picture Only

Let's make a few overlaps in the Rubin Cut 1 sequence (or your copy of it) that we reviewed at the end of Chapter 2. There are many ways to directly execute a rolling trim, but let's do it the most conservative way as a means of explanation.

I'm demonstrating with a shot that comes between where Kirsten asks for a second time "Do you love me?" (1G-5) and Chris replies "yes" (1A-2). (About 27 seconds into the sequence.)

First, lock both sound tracks by clicking on the Lock icon in the Track Controls for A1 and A2. This prevents the audio from changing in any way when we do our adjustments.

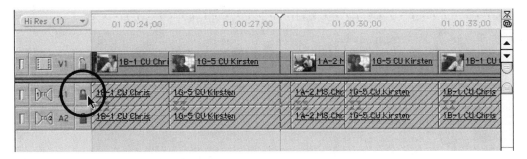

1 Double-click a transition you want to adjust.

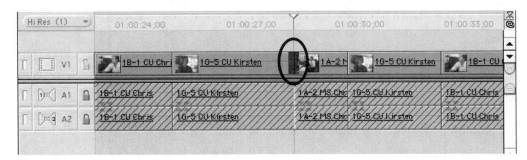

Remember, this is a trim. The only difference between this one and one we did in the last chapter is that it is critical we don't change the overall duration of the picture track while the sound is locked. *Rolling* trims do this. Ripple trims (like in Chapter 2) do not. Look for those green bars on both sides. Look for the rolling trim icon.

For a rolling trim, make sure the green bar appears over both sides of the Trim Edit window.

2 Play either side of the cut; you'll see that you can select and shuttle each side independently.

3 Go to the shot of Kirsten on the A-side, and adjust the Out point to start a second or so earlier. When you mark a new Out point, the other shot will move automatically to correspond to the change in the shot you played. Notice the Timeline representations shift also, but still remain in sync.

Now let's see what Chris is doing on the B-side (the right side of the Trim Edit window).

It looks like he's listening to her speak. He seems serious. Good. The overlap works, and I think it improves this moment.

Look at the Timeline. Notice that clip 1G-5 is now sort of L-shaped. It fits perfectly together with clip 1A-2. And all the shots after this still have their straight cuts. This is a successful rolling trim execution.

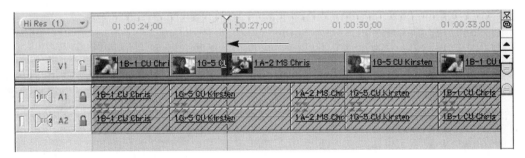

A Rolling Shortcut

There's another way to execute a rolling trim, which I want to show you (and in the process we'll adjust the one we just made). This method doesn't use the Trim Edit window (and consequently can be a little fly-by-night), but I want to show it mostly so you can better visualize the rolling process.

Play the part of this scene we've been working on, where Kirsten says "I'll ask you again, do you love me?" and Chris says (more hesitantly) "yes." Stop the playhead in the middle of the B-side (the shot of Chris), but after the overlap has occurred.

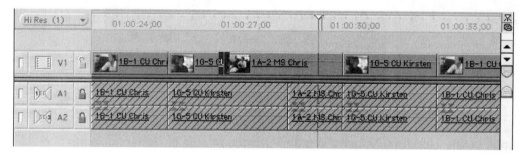

Rather than double-clicking the edit to bring up the Trim window (as before), go to the toolbox and get the Rolling Trim tool.

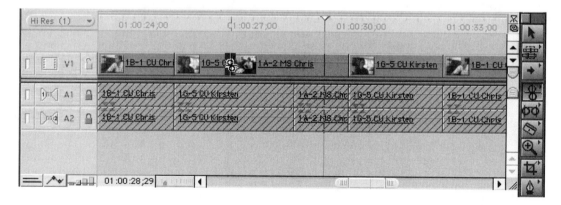

Now click and hold on the transition, and a different sort of trim window appears.

This is the Canvas version of a trim window (called the Two-up Display). It's not as full-featured as the real Trim Edit window, but it will show you what you are doing. When you're using the Rolling Trim tool from the toolbox, it means you're making the trim predominantly in the Timeline. You will likely be using the playhead to help identify where you are trimming the cut point "to."

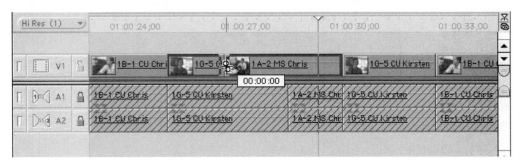

Notice that in the Timeline you can slide the picture cut point back and forth to any location you like. This really drives home the "rolling" nature of the rolling trim. As you move left and right from the place you started, a small box (called a Tool Tip) appears to show you how many frames (plus, to the right; minus to the left) you have changed the cut point.

Watch out: You can roll a shot clear out of the timeline. I like to choose one shot or the other and make that my "main" focus as I try an overlap. In this case, I know I want to choose the Out point based on Kirsten's line. I want her talking. I want her eyes open. And I don't want her shot made too short. When I mark a new out (-1:22), I feel I've addressed those initial concerns.

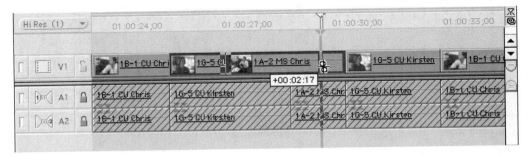

Rolled to the right.

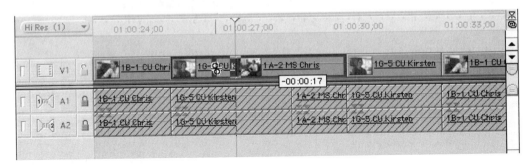

Rolled to the left.

You may also notice as you roll around that the edit point you are holding in your hands (click-hold-drag) is snapping between points: from the location of the original sound transition to the playhead, and so on. Because snapping is *on*, this tool lets you precisely roll to likely spots for the trim, or even to return an overlap to a straight cut. If you want to roll to a position other than a marked (and snapping-friendly) spot, you may need to turn snapping *off* to execute the trim. We'll leave it on for now because snapping is a powerful force in the Macintosh editing world.

FCP actually has another way to perform this rolling trim edit function: It's called Extend Edit. I don't think it merits memorization as long as you understand what you are doing. More important, it also has a keyboard shortcut, which is good for professionals but not really necessary for you. Select a cut. Stop playing the master at the spot where you want the edit and press E on the keyboard. Cool.

Here's a review of the Rolling Shortcut method:

1 Shuttle around in the sequence to the precise spot you think you want the transition to occur.

2 Get the Rolling Trim tool from the toolbox.

3 Click and drag the edit point toward the playhead. It will snap to your parked location, and presto, the edit point has rolled to this spot.

Rolling trims are great. More than 90 percent of all my rolling trims are picture-only. As you'll come to see, you will almost never perform them in sound alone.

The Insert

As you may recall from our vocabulary lessons in Chapter 1, in general, any time you add a clip to a sequence in FCP, you're "inserting" it. We did a fair amount of inserts back in the last chapter. Inserts, like trims, benefit from a non-rippling variation. A non-rippling insert is perhaps the crux of sophisticated-looking editing. In FCP, the non-rippling insert is called an overwrite edit. The icons for the overwrite edit are colored red because FCP knows there is a reasonable risk that you'll write over something you didn't intend to write over. But I don't consider them dangerous.

There are many reasons to execute an overwrite insert in just video or just audio. In picture alone, an overwrite can be used to insert a reaction shot of someone listening over a shot of someone speaking. In sound alone, it can be used to cover over a bit of audio you don't like (like an airplane flying overhead or the director speaking off-camera). When you're really skilled, audio-only overwrites can be used to replace single words or parts of words marred by a bad performance. Let's learn about the overwrite.

Three- and Four-Point Editing

Ahh, but first a digression. Early in their education, serious students of editing face the often-confusing concept of three- and four-point editing. It's a little like explaining how to tie your shoes. It's hard to say in words, but it's fairly obvious once someone shows you. Hang on.

All shots in a sequence can be described using two key pieces of information: first, what portion of a source clip is being used, and second, precisely where it is placed in the sequence. It takes two specific pieces of data to describe each of those things: its In point and its Out point. Thus, every edit can be written down as four data points:

Source: In   Source: Out
(the beginning and end of the shot)

Master: In   Master: Out
(its location in the Timeline)

To make an edit, any edit, exactly three of these four pieces of information must be known. Another way of saying this is that if you have three of the above data points, you can always figure out the fourth.

These are the "points" being referred to in the expression "three- and four-point editing."

Why haven't we talked about this before—I mean, we're in Chapter 3 and we've done a fair amount of editing without much "point" discussion? Because modern editing systems like FCP tend to hide all this point stuff except when you really need it. You recall that we marked an In and Out in the source material prior to inserting. (Or that FCP always sees at least two points in the clip—whether you place them or not?) These are two of the points. FCP always knows the first two points. You can change them, but they're always there.

But what of the third point? I did say you must have three to edit. The third point is always *where the playhead is parked*. When you make an insert, unless otherwise specified, the playhead denotes the third point. That's why we've been able to edit making only two marks in the Viewer.

But there comes a time when those three points aren't the three you want to use.

Overwrite (Non-Rippling Insert) in Picture Only

Let's say someone is talking in a shot that has been cut into your sequence. It's a fairly long boring shot of them ranting on and on, and you want to see someone else (known in the biz as a "cut-away" or "reaction shot"). You want to specify a place in the sequence where the cut-away would begin, and you want to note where it should end. You do these by using the Mark In and Mark Out buttons—but in the *Canvas* (or Timeline), not in the Viewer.

Let's try it.

Assuming you've been following along, you're still looking at Rubin's Cut 1 (or your copy of it) in the Timeline and Canvas. If it's not up now, open it up.

1   Play into the long rant by Kirsten. She is saying "I found these next to the bed," and she is holding out something we can't see.

2 Lock the sound tracks. In truth, you could do this at any point before you actually execute the insert, but it's good to do it as soon as you think of it.

I want to see the bag Kirsten is holding, but I don't want to interrupt her speech. So I am going to play the sequence and mark an In and Out to show where I want a shot to go.

Notice the In and Out marks in the scale of the Timeline. This is the range where I want to place a shot. I already have a vague idea of what shot goes here; now, to find it.

3 Go to the Browser and find the bag shot called 1J. Double-click it and watch it in the Viewer. There's lots of interesting material here. What you're looking for is an *area* of good material.

4 When you find it, stop on the first frame of that area and mark an In. I like this one:

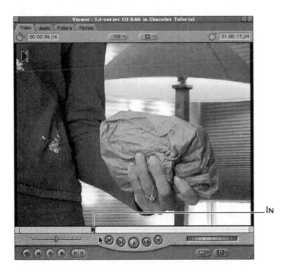

If you pause and look around at the Viewer and the Canvas, you will see three points: one on the source side and two on the master side. This is all that is required to make an edit.

5 Now you're going to do an overwrite edit (a "non-rippling insert") in picture only. Drag the new shot in the Viewer onto the Canvas and drop it onto the red Overwrite box.

After you drop the shot into the Canvas, the Timeline reflects the cut-away.

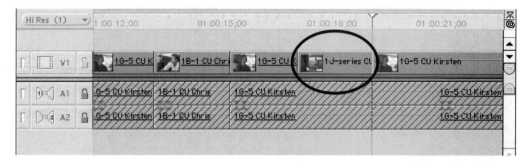

Three-point edits do not always have to be an In on the source and an In and Out on the master. There are four permutations of this three-point editing.

1 You know what the insert (reaction or cut-away) shot is going to be (source In and Out), and you know where it must start in the sequence (master In).

2 You know what the insert shot is going to be (source In and Out), and you know where it must end in the sequence (master Out); this is some-times called "backtiming."

3 You know where the insert needs to be placed (master In and Out), and you know where the source material must start (source In); this is what we just did.

4 You know where the insert needs to be placed (master In and Out), and you know where the source material must end (source Out); this is another variation on backtiming.

Experiment with cut-aways in the picture track for a while before moving on. You want to be comfortable with these functions before we do them in sound, where they are harder to visualize.

Overwrite (Non-Rippling Insert) in Sound Only

In picture, overwrites are easy; you can see what you are doing. In sound they are less obvious, but still easy.

Let's replace sound in one of the shots, and do it with a sound-only overwrite, using your knowledge of three-point edits.

In the third shot of Rubin's Cut 1, you can hear me talking to Chris. I like his expression, but it's too bad I'm talking. In many cases you'd reject using this shot because the sound is wrong. But that would be a shame.

1 Before you forget, lock the *picture* track (V1) and unlock the *sound* (A1 and A2).

   While we could replace the *entire* audio from 1C-1 (from the head to the tail of the shot), let's practice by just replacing the worst part.

2 Play through Chris's shot 1C-1 and stop before you hear the director (me) talking. Mark an In point.

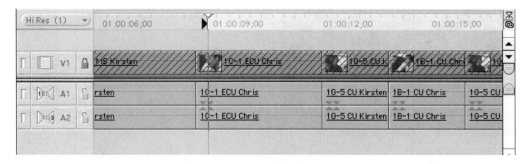

3 Play until the bad sound ends, and mark an Out.

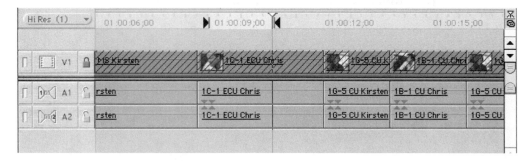

Now that you have determined what material to remove, let's try a couple different options.

First, ambience. Ambience is production sound recorded during your shoot, when no one is talking or making any sounds. It is the "ambient sound" of the room—also called "room tone." Where do you find ambience to use? With experience you would know to record it while you were on location. If you hadn't learned that (or forgot to), the next best trick is to find a pause in a recorded take and hope it's long enough to fill the space you need. Since we only need a second or two, I'll bet we can find what we need.

If you give up, I found a bit here in 1C-1:

Always start hunting in the take you are in, for the best match of sound. Look near the slate or at the end of the take.

1 In 1C-1 (or wherever you found some ambience) mark an In. I'm just estimating that I have enough pure ambience, without someone talking, starting from this point. We'll find out soon enough.

2 Now perform an overwrite in the Canvas. The shot will drop into the space you created with the marks, and will only affect the sound tracks. It should look something like this:

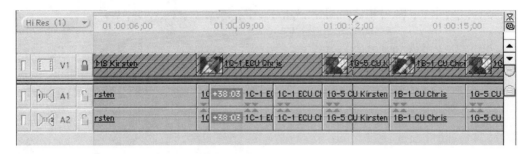

A second way to remove material is "to slug" it; that is, to cut something out and replace it with a piece of black filler, called (of course) "slug." In picture you'd see black, in sound, it's just silence. There are a few ways to do this, but in keeping with our experimentation in overwrite inserts, we're first going to need to learn about a new kind of source material.

In the Viewer, there is a small button at the bottom of the window that brings up a menu that allows you to switch the source material from video you've collected in the Browser to specialty video that FCP makes for you. Because FCP is generating this source material for you, it's called the Generator menu.

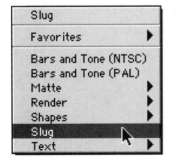

1 Open the Generator menu. As you can see, there are several kinds of specialized source material that FCP will generate for you, including titles, color bars, mattes, and shapes for special effects. The only one I want to use now is "slug." There are some subtle differences between putting slug in your sequence, and just having nothing there (a gap), but we'll save that discussion.

2 For now, just select the slug source, and watch it pop up in the Viewer.

You'll see the sprockets on the left side of the window, indicating that this is the beginning of the roll of slug. FCP gives you two minutes of slug here to work with. You'll only need a tiny bit.

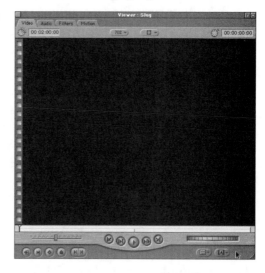

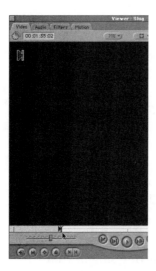

3 Now that this source material is here, mark an In somewhere in the slug. You could just mark the first frame. I tend to click a little bit farther in (it's an old-but-good habit of not ever using the "first" frame of any shot).

4 Back in the Timeline, we're starting with the ambience (from 1C-1) we rolled in a few moments ago. Move to the head of this shot and mark an In point; move to the tail and mark an Out.

This can be done using the screen commands  or keyboard commands ⬆ I ⬇ O or if you want to get fancy, there is a special button on the screen that does exactly this, when the playhead is over the clip you want to mark—Mark Clip.

However you get there, when you're done, your Timeline will look like this:

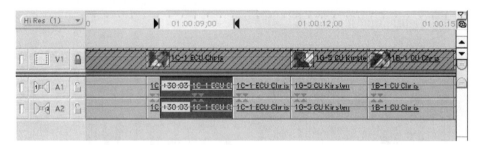

In case you haven't been counting, this makes three points (one in the source, two in the master).

5 Drag the slug into the Canvas and overwrite this sound.

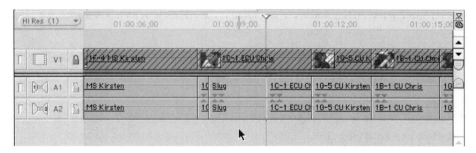

Using a slug is a fallback position when you don't have good ambience or don't have the time to go looking for it. But you will notice that the sound of silence is actually quite different from the ambience in the production, and the abrupt change can be as jarring as a bad edit.

Undo the slug and put the ambience back in. We'll work on the sound later.

Adjusting Your One-Track Shots

Once the video-only or sound-only insert is in place, there are lots of ways to adjust it. What you're going to find, however, is that as you move into more one-track modifications, your Timeline is going to start to get complicated. What was once simple, clear straight cuts (with all the sound neatly fitting under each picture shot), becomes a patchwork of picture and sound (overlaps, inserts of picture not linking to sound, inserts of sound chopping up tracks). Any editor, no matter how seasoned, would start to get slightly queasy when it came time to make changes to a Timeline that looked like this:

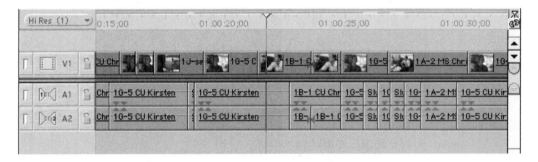

But if you work to keep things in sync as you go, and move slowly when learning about these adjustments, the gradually growing complexity of the Timeline will be manageable.

Rolling Edit, Part 2 (Trimming an Insert)

Any time you want to adjust a shot in either picture or sound only, it must be a rolling (non-rippling) modification. This will guarantee you never lose sync between picture and sound tracks. You used the rolling trim to create overlaps earlier in this chapter. It is just as simple to adjust an insert using the rolling trim.

Since you're so familiar with rolling trims, I won't demonstrate how to do them here. But I encourage you to try one. If you find rolling trims are still a challenge, this a good time to go back and practice them until they're second nature.

Lift (Non-Ripple Delete)

We used Delete (with and without rippling) in the last chapter to tighten shots or get rid of unwanted material. We can do this in picture or sound alone as well, but we'll need to mind the sync.

Let's try an adjustment with a Lift (a delete that doesn't ripple). The easy way to do this is simply to select the picture-only or sound-only shot you don't like, and press Delete.

1 Make sure the picture track is locked.

2 Select the ambient sound shot you inserted a few moments ago.

3 Now press the Delete key.

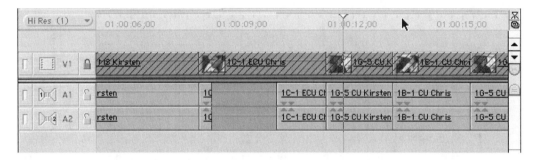

This certainly gets rid of the sound. Since you didn't ripple, the hole just sits there, and there is no sound while it plays. You'll notice that the gap you have left has many of the same properties as the slug you inserted earlier. It is considered bad form in basic editing to leave gaps in your sequence, but you can see how easy it is to remove material from your sequence and still keep the following shots in place, held in sync.

But there are some other tools for adjusting inserts as well. The inventors of computerized editing systems came up with some clever "macros" to adjust shots in your sequence. These are no different from the basics you've been learning, but they combine a number of steps, with elegant results. Slip and Slide are simply variations on ripple trims, doing two ripple trims at the same time. And they are great for making small adjustments of cut-away shots—particularly picture-only cut-away shots!

Slide

Slide is an elegant and magical tool. Imagine that your insert shot is not glued into the Timeline, but floating above it, like this:

The Slide tool allows you to grab hold of the clip, and move it (*slide* it) around in the Timeline to occur earlier or later in the sequence. Here's how it works in FCP.

1 In the sequence, find our insert shot of the bag in Kirsten's hand (1J) and select it with the Arrow tool.

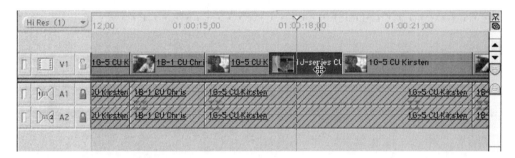

Actually, you didn't need to select the shot to do the slide, but I wanted you to see what it looks like when selected, as compared to when you're about to slide.

2 Go to the toolbox and get the Slide tool (if it's not immediately visible, it's under the Slip tool—click and hold to bring up other options for this toolbox position).

Once you've selected the Slide tool, use it to click on this insert shot and select it.

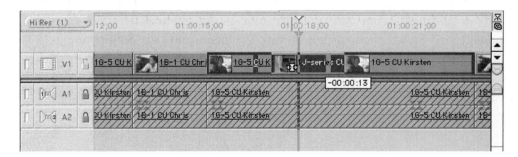

3 Click and hold on the insert shot. You'll see two now-familiar features pop up. First, the Canvas turns into the special two-up display. But rather than showing you the two frames at the edit point (as it does when you're trimming), it shows you the two frames of the tail and head around the insert shot. Since, presumably, you know what your insert looks like (it's a bag), and you're not changing it, there's no need to show it to you. On the other hand, as you slide the clip around, this dual display will show you the frames to which the clip will now attach on either end.

The other familiar feature is the little tool tip window, where the number of frames you've slid the shot are indicated (which I call the "shift-offset").

4 Slide the shot to the left a little bit. According to my tool tip window, I've moved -0:13; moving left is negative, so I just shifted the shot to the left 13 frames, or just under half a second.

5 Let go here and the Canvas will return to normal, and the insert shot will be moved to its new location.

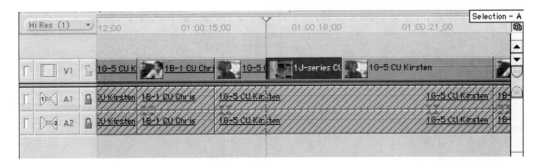

Technically, Slide does not change the In or Out of the insert shot, but it does move the In (and Out) of where the shot goes in the sequence. Most beginners will find the Slide function intuitively obvious to use.

Slip

Unlike Slide, Slipping takes a little more effort to understand.

 This time, instead of visualizing the insert shot floating above the Timeline, imagine a hole in your sequence where the insert shot was, with the insert *underneath* the Timeline and moving around. Slipping a shot means moving the video you see in the hole, without changing or moving the hole itself.

Now the clip is underneath the Timeline. You can move it around, but you can only see the part that is visible through the hole.

It is as if you said to yourself "This is where I want something to go, but this shot isn't exactly the bit of source material I want."

As with Slide, you can Slip a shot by grabbing the Slip Edit tool from the toolbox and clicking and dragging a shot to left or right. The graphical representation of the clip in the Timeline won't appear to move as you drag, but in the two-up display you'll see that the video underneath is adjusted.

Go back to the insert of the bag in Kirsten's hand. When you click and hold this shot with the Slip Edit tool, you'll see the Canvas change into the two-up display, showing you the head (left) and tail (right) of the insert.

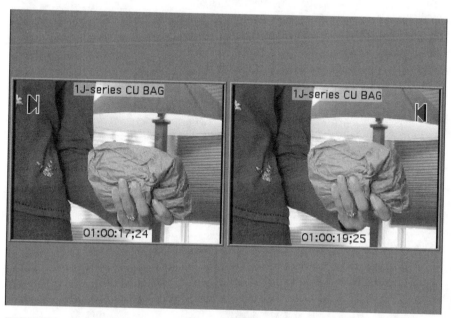

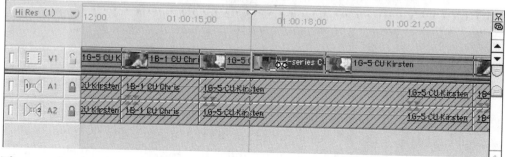

The counter-intuitive thing about slipping is that as you drag the shot to the left, you are actually beginning the insert *later* (it feels as if moving to the left should start the insert earlier). As you drag to the right (as I did here), you'll see the shift-offset window indicate that you are moving plus frames, and the shot shifts backward on the Canvas. Pause for a moment, and just think about this. I'll wait here.

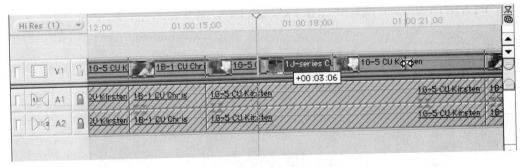

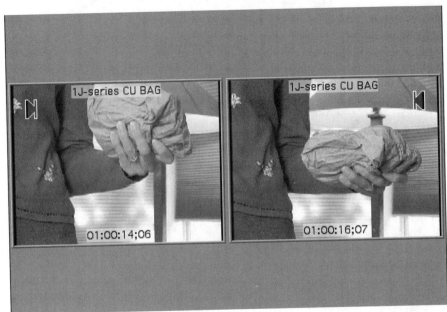

It's natural for Westerners to associate moving to the right with moving forward—we read left to right. But when you drag and pull the insert to the right, you are moving the start frame of the shot earlier and earlier into the original clip. Watch the timecode numbers FCP shows you in the Canvas head and tail frames—they will always help you orient yourself as to which way you are moving the insert.

When you're done, let go. The Canvas returns to normal and the Timeline reflects the changed source material. Oddly enough, since the shot hasn't changed its Timeline location, the window will look pretty much the way it did when you started.

Moving Shots Around

When digital editing systems were first being released just over a decade ago, they often came from users who were frustrated with making demo tapes—a task that requires doing something quite difficult in videotape editing: moving shots around. Say you have three shots—one, two, and three. They are in a row, and you think, "Hey, I should put three right after one." You would simply want to grab three, drag it to between one and two, and let go. But as you may have seen from even these basic editing tutorials, editing isn't really much about shuffling shots around. As neat a feature as this is, in narrative material you don't do it all that often.

Still, for many kinds of projects you'll want to do it, and you should understand how it works. This is technically known as "timeline trimming." It means you're making edits and changes by looking at the graphical display and adjusting relationships there, like rearranging slides. You don't even need to watch the video itself to make these decisions.

As you could probably guess, the essence of moving shots around involves these steps:

1 Select a shot.

2 Click and drag it to a new location.

3 Let go when it's in the right place.

These can be described more specifically in the terms we have been using in this chapter and the last: Ripple delete a shot from one place and then ripple insert it back into the sequence someplace else. FCP uses the terms *overwrite* and *swap* when you drag clips already in the Timeline around to new locations. Of course, FCP will want to know where to do the insert, and it will want to know if this is a ripple or non-ripple adjustment.

1 Go to the sequence you've been working on and click and drag the shot of Chris fumbling with his ring. Right now, the sequence goes from Kirsten, to Chris saying nothing, to a shot of Chris fumbling with his ring, then back to Kirsten.

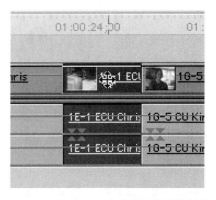

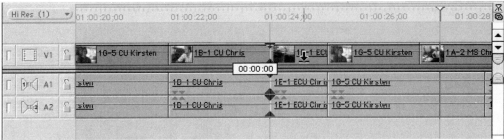

If you just drag the ring shot to a new location and let go, FCP will delete the shot from its original location without rippling, leaving a gap, and insert this shot by overwriting wherever you let go. If you're trying to swap the ring shot and the shot of Chris saying nothing (going from A-B to B-A), this won't work.

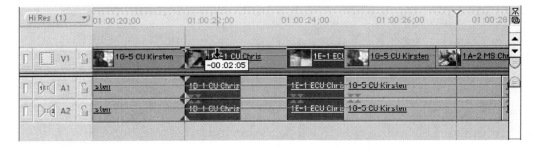

2 Go ahead and play with this. As soon as you drag the clip even a few frames, notice the Overwrite icon (the down arrow) appears, telling you that you're in overwrite (non-rippling) mode. The down arrow is saying, in effect, "this shot is going right here, over this." The shadow of the clip you're dragging is solid and dark.

3 Just for the record, I've never needed to make this particular modification. Undo it.

4 Exactly as before, click and drag the ring shot to the edit point after Kirsten and before Chris, but don't let go. While you're dragging, hold down the Option key. The cursor changes from the Overwrite icon into a Swap Insert icon, and the shadow of the shot you're dragging changes into an outline.

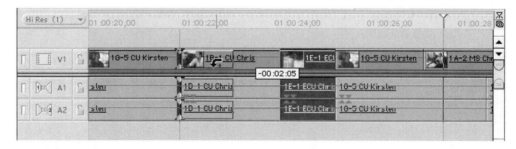

5 Now when you let go, the B-shot moves to before the A-shot, and the A-shot shoves down into the space left by the B-shot. There are no gaps, and the two shots have changed positions. In other words, the gap was ripple deleted and the B-shot was ripple inserted into its new location in one simple move.

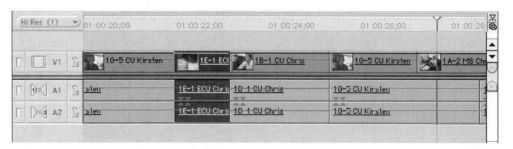

You could do this all day, reorganizing shots like cards in a poker hand. As I said before, it doesn't come up all that often, but it does come up—particularly in non-narrative material (stuff without a script). I have one warning, and it's the reason I'd suggest avoiding swap edits: There are a number of odd occurrences you trigger when you're holding down the Option key while working in the Timeline. If you don't press it at just the right moment, you might get confused about what exactly happened. The Option key has many uses in FCP, and you'll probably make some mistakes while practicing swap edits, but you'll end up learning a few handy new tricks in the process:

- To do a swap edit easily, just remember not to press the Option key until you get the clip to its new location and are almost ready to let go.

- Press Option *before* you click and drag the clip and you'll copy the shot you're moving. The original stays put and the copy goes to the new location.

- When you drop the copy of the clip in its new location, you'll do either an overwrite or an insert, depending on when you let go of the Option key and the clip.

I recommend that you practice these Option key moves in a duplicate sequence that you can delete when you're done, because it can take a little practice to get your timing right. Have fun. But don't say I didn't warn you.

Life In and Out of Sync

Everything we have been doing in picture-only or sound-only was executed carefully, so as not to go out of sync: Rolling trims of picture only, overwrites of sound, ripple deletes of linked picture and sound. All prevent you from ever losing that precious relationship known as "sync."

But going out of sync, in controlled situations, is not all that bad. Sometimes losing sync is a necessary step in a multi-staged solution to some problem. Film editors are particularly good at coming and going from sync effortlessly. It was only with the advent of videotape editing that editors became so stressed out about moving the sync relationship around to fix a problem. As an editor, you really want to start getting comfortable moving in and out of sync; it's an important stage. Hang on.

Let's do a ripple trim in picture only.

1 Lock the sound tracks.

2 Go get the Ripple Trim tool from the toolbox.

3 Double-click an edit point and adjust the B-side alone just a few frames. As you remove frames from one side of the cut and not the other, you can see what's coming.

Cut seems OK? It's not.

You're out of sync. Let's take a look at the Timeline.

It's a little hard to see with the sound tracks still locked, but FCP puts a big red notice on any picture shot that is out of sync with its production sound. In this case, we took 10 frames off the head of the picture, so from there through the end of the sequence, *all* pictures are 10 frames out of sync—the move rippled clear through to the end.

If we look closer (and unlock sound tracks for clarity) you can see the tell-tale footprint of a shot out of sync. This is useful because when something is out of sync you need to discern exactly where it *first* went out of sync in order to fix it.

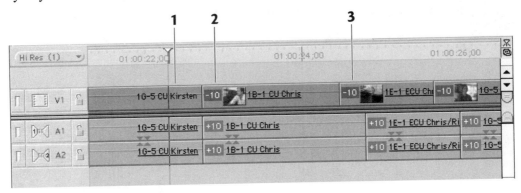

1 Find that last shot that is still in sync. Here it is (10-5 CU Kirsten); it ends with a straight cut.

2 Here's the place we did the trim. It's a little deceptive because this shot also begins with a straight cut, but that's only because we did the trim and all the shots afterward rippled into the hole created by the 10-frame shortfall. The warning in the Timeline says the picture is -10 frames, or 10 frames shorter than the sound. It also says the sound is

+10 frames, or 10 frames longer than the picture. FCP doesn't care how you fix it. Put 10 frames back in picture, or take 10 out of sound. It won't judge you.

> If you're advanced, Final Cut also has more automated ways to restore sync, using contextual menus. You can investigate those once you've mastered this manual approach.

3 Here's the first shot that actually *looks* out of sync in the Timeline. Like an earthquake, the picture track has slid, and you'll see the pattern created in straight cuts when all of them are rippled to the same extent.

If you're like most editors, you'll simply hit Undo and perform your trim again, this time being careful to roll both sides evenly. But you could choose to be more selective about where the 10 frames you need to adjust are going to come from. You could, for instance, do a series of small rippling trims, some in picture and some in sound, so that the net result is a resynchronization of picture and sound.

For instance, you could

1 Remove four frames of sound here using the Razor Blade tool and ripple delete. Now we're only six frames out of sync.

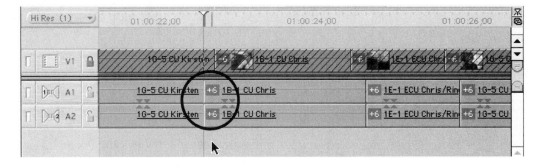

2 Remove three frames of sound here where no one is talking, again using the Razor Blade tool and ripple delete.

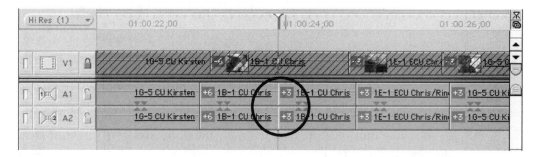

3 Lock the sound and turn on the picture, then perform a trim of the picture only, adding in three more frames.

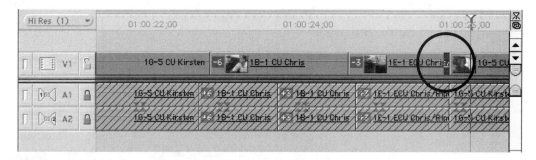

As you perform the trims you can actually *see* the frames being added to the Timeline and the out of sync warning number getting smaller and smaller until it is gone.

Now your Timeline contains some unusual cuts. It's in sync for awhile, then there are a couple of slightly out of sync areas, then it goes back into sync. While this isn't wonderful editing form, sometimes this kind of repair work is necessary as you try to solve various creative problems that only editing can solve. In this particular case, the two shots that are a few frames out of sync contain no talking in the sound track—they are basically picture-only shots with ambient sound. Consequently, there is no problem aesthetically.

I intentionally go out of sync and then get myself back only when I'm re-editing and I decide that there's simply too long a pause in the sound track and I want to pull it out. In sound-only, I use the Razor Blade tool and ripple delete to remove a second or so of unwanted silence.

Now I'm out of sync by the length of the sound I removed. To get back in sync, I need to remove picture from *somewhere* before anyone starts talking again. In this example, I pulled out sound beneath the insert of the bag. Now, I'll use a rippling trim to remove picture: a little from the bag insert,

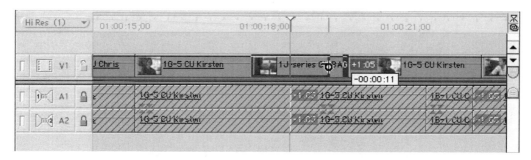

and a little more from the head of Kirsten's continuing dialog shot.

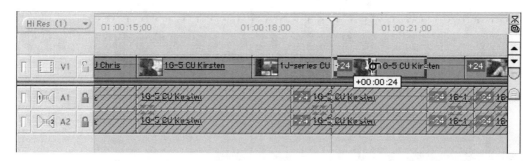

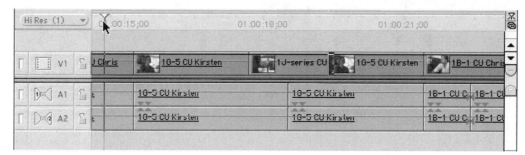

Done. It looks pretty much the same as when we started.

And now you're back in sync, but with a tighter track.

The Sound Mix

Once you understand how three-point edits work in sound, you have begun your experience as a "sound editor." In Hollywood filmmaking, the "editor" is responsible primarily for the picture cut and the associated "production sound"—the sync sound shot on location. While a picture editor might use the occasional sound effect or some music to rough something together, specialists eventually complete these refinements. There are sound editors, dialog editors, music editors, and effects editors. There are people whose jobs include putting all these tracks together and making sure the volume of each is appropriate for what is happening in the movie (sound mixers).

FCP is a post-production tool—not just an "editing system." As an FCP user, and a student of holistic video, you can handle the picture cut, but you can also manage the audio editing, the mixing, the color correction of picture, the special effects and titles without getting up from your chair. While we are dedicated here to getting a good picture-cutting foundation, you'll want to know enough to "sell your cut"; that is, to show a producer or director (or spouse) that your picture cut is done, even if the sound work and other finishing touches are not. This takes some basic skills in audio editing and mixing.

Adjusting Audio Levels

The goal of an audio mix is to make material produced from a wide range of audio recording conditions become a single, seamless soundtrack. Adjusting audio levels the way a sound mixer does is a simple, but important, first step into the realm of making a "sellable" picture cut.

When video is recorded on location, the microphone on the camera records production sound. Every time you move the camera, the volume of the sound may change, as well as the degree of noise the microphone picks up from the surroundings.

If I am recording you from far away, and I turn up the volume to hear you better, I am also increasing the volume of the background noise. If I am recording you close up, I don't need to increase the volume much to get a nice, clear signal, so I have probably picked up very little background noise.

In FCP you can adjust the volume (actually the power) of each shot individually or of an entire track. It's called adjusting the Levels. And like everything in FCP, there's a keyboard way to do it and an on-screen method. Let's start with the on-screen method, in the Timeline.

If you look at the embedded controls in the frame of the Timeline, the second one you come to, at the bottom left, is the audio level controller—called the Clip Overlays Controller.

When you click on this box, you reveal a red line down the middle of your audio tracks. As your cursor moves over this red line, the cursor changes into an adjuster—raising or lowering this line as you click and drag.

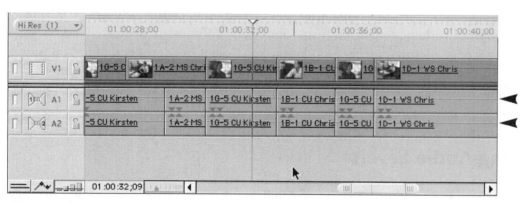

It's hard to see in black-and-white. I'll try to point it out, but it's better to experiment on your own.

In the sound tracks, this level line is used to raise and lower the volume of the shot. (Oddly, there is a similar *black* line in picture, and moving it raises and lowers the opacity of a shot.)

What we call "volume" is actually a function of acoustic or electrical power and is measured in decibels (abbreviated dB). Decibels are on a logarithmic scale, which simply means that a large degree of measurement (and user control) has been squeezed into a condensed range of numbers. Thus, it doesn't usually take an adjustment of too many decibels to even out the mix of different takes. One dB is about the smallest discernable change in volume. Making an adjustment to the decibel levels is sometimes called "adjusting the gain."

If you want to raise or lower the volume of a number of shots, select the shots you want to adjust, and go to the Modify menu.

There are two important choices here.

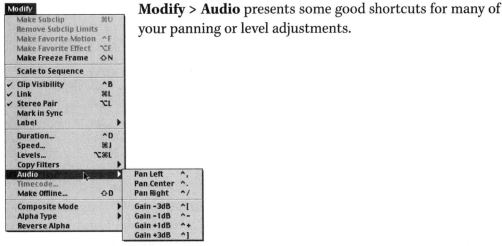

Modify > Audio presents some good shortcuts for many of your panning or level adjustments.

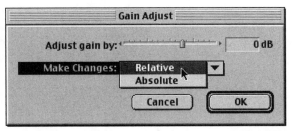

Modify > Levels brings up a window where you can adjust either the absolute or relative volume of the selected shots.

Modify > Levels is a little more technical than the Modify > Audio choices. "Absolute level" sets all selected shots to precisely the same dB, no matter what their levels were when you started the modification. "Relative levels" moves all the selected shots up or down a given dB from their starting position.

Sometimes it's best for amateurs with little time to work on video projects to skip messing with levels, and simply add audio cross fades at transitions where there is a discernable change in room ambience. You could spend as much (or more) time working on sound as on picture.

Audio Cross Fade

An audio cross fade turns down the volume on the first shot over a short period of time (the default is 1 second), while simultaneously turning up the volume on the B-side over the same period. One fades out, the other fades in. I like to think of these as a poor man's mix. Often, when two shots simply have different-sounding audio and I don't feel like spending a lot of time playing with the various advanced FCP features for tweaking audio (volume, pan, EQ, DeEssing, Pass Filtering, and so on), I just add an audio cross fade across the transition to soften any differences. About 75 percent of the time this works like a charm.

> I don't do this, by the way, until I am otherwise done working on my edit. All these cross fades obscure the audio tracks and visually complicate re-editing. But they are easy enough to add or remove as required, so if you have a cross fade that is bothering you, just delete it until later.

Let's go back to the sequence we've been working on one last time. Cue up to the beginning and start playing it.

Even between the first two shots, there is an appreciable level change from one to the next. If you want to de-emphasize the edit, soften the change.

Now we're going somewhere we've never been before: the Effects tab in the Browser. Click on the tab and you'll see an assortment of folders. The one we want to open is labeled Audio Transitions.

1 Click and drag "Cross Fade (+3dB)" onto the audio transition between the first two shots of the sequence and let go.

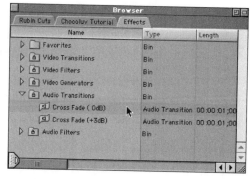

2 Now play across the transition, listening carefully.

3 Undo the cross fade and play across the transition again, to note the difference.

4 Use the Redo command (Command-Y) to put the cross fade back in.

5 Play across the transition one more time, to train your ear to hear the subtle differences between an audio cross fade and a straight cut.

Note that there are two default cross fades offered: 0dB and +3dB. These are highly simplified names for some sophisticated audio manipulations. I generally use the +3dB option when going from take to take in similar-sounding shots, and I use the 0dB version when the shifts are larger, say from one scene to a completely different scene. The bottom line is that you should just try them. If one works, great; if it sounds odd, try the other.

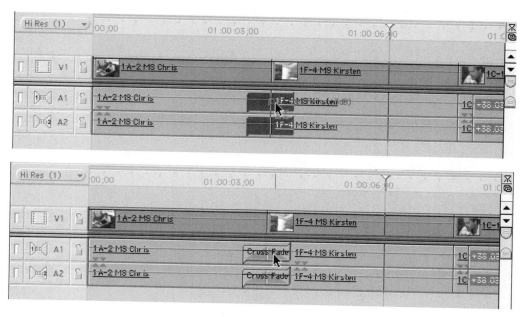

That helps a little. (It helps even more if you raise the audio level a few dB in the first shot as well!) In some ways, adding a cross fade is like making a short overlap, moving the sound and picture edits away from each other.

We won't spend any more time here on audio cross fades. But they are your first step in transition effects and foreshadow our work in the next chapter on fancier things, like more detailed work in tracks and effects.

We've worked hard in this chapter to keep our separate picture and sound tracks in sync with each other. Without learning any new concepts, we applied Trim, Insert, and Delete (both ripple and non-ripple varieties) to picture-only, sound-only, and both together. And we've learned these embody virtually every function a professional film editor would ever need. While there are shortcuts to most of these features, you might never have to learn them if you didn't want to.

Now that you have editing down (and I'm not being flip when I say that you know enough now to edit a feature film if you wanted to), let's take a look at some of the "bells and whistles" editors often use to finish their projects.

CHAPTER 4 Fancy Stuff

One of the wonderful things about Final Cut Pro is how easily it combines sounds and pictures together on multiple video and audio tracks to spiff up your project. Although you manipulate picture and sound in pretty much the same way using FCP, it's best (at least at first) to think of them separately. Mixing images together on multiple video tracks elevates simple editing to a level generically known as "special effects," or more technically as "compositing." This tends to require rendering, and dramatically slows down your workflow. Adding audio tracks, on the other hand, produces real-time results—in most cases, FCP can play up to eight channels of audio simultaneously, and with simple processing, can add as many as 99 tracks.

In the last chapter you learned techniques for treating picture and sound separately. In this chapter you'll build on that foundation by adding additional picture and sound tracks.

Customizing Your Interface

Let's begin by looking at the ways FCP allows you to prepare your workspace specifically for the tasks at hand. When you launch FCP for the first time, you're presented with the default (or "standard") interface arrangement, which presents each FCP window in its typical, average proportions.

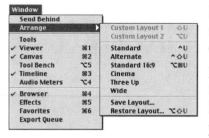

But each of the four primary windows can be resized and repositioned according to the kind of work you do, the size of your display, and your personal aesthetic preferences. There are a handful of variations you might want to consider. FCP has some preconfigured layouts prepared for your editing pleasure, nestled within the Window menu. You can start with those or experiment on your own. I'd like to show you a couple window layouts I've seen and used that I think make the work of editing more clear and efficient.

Formats for Editing

The Timeline is one of the most critical aspects of the display. Often, you'll want it to occupy the maximum horizontal space across the screen. Because most television and movie editors are principally concerned with one (or maybe two) picture tracks and two (or maybe four) sound tracks, their timeline does not need to get much larger vertically: three to six tracks usually fit nicely in the default height.

If you want to see more than will fit without scrolling the Timeline window up and down, there is a height control button embedded in the Timeline window frame, where you can enlarge or minimize the track height at will.

The Browser, however, can be much smaller. As you may have noticed in prior chapters, the Browser need only list the names of shots to be useful. So my first suggested reconfiguration of the interface resizes the Timeline and Browser:

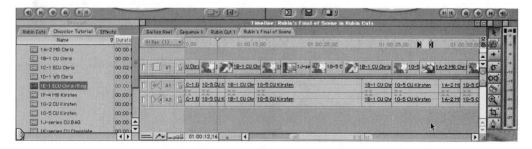

In truth, Hollywood editing bays tend to run two computer displays at a time. When placed side-by-side, the left display is dedicated *entirely* to the Browser. This allows the right display to show only the Timeline and the Viewer/Canvas.

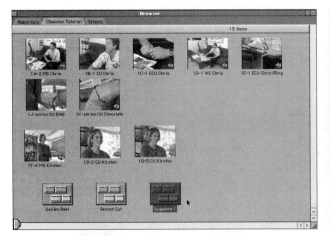

Here are two side-by-side monitors with our Chocoluv Tutorial. When the Browser is used full-screen in this way, editors also tend to look at clips as icons or "picons" (short for "picture icons").

In the next chapter we'll look at organizing clips and sequences, and you'll see further ways this full-screen browser might be organized.

Formats for Effects

You might want to alter your default interface if you're working on something that specifically demands a different workflow. If you plan, for instance, to use many special effects, the length of the Timeline may be less important than its height, and space for the Effects window and a Video Scope (to adjust technical parameters of the image) become more important, resulting in a configuration more like this:

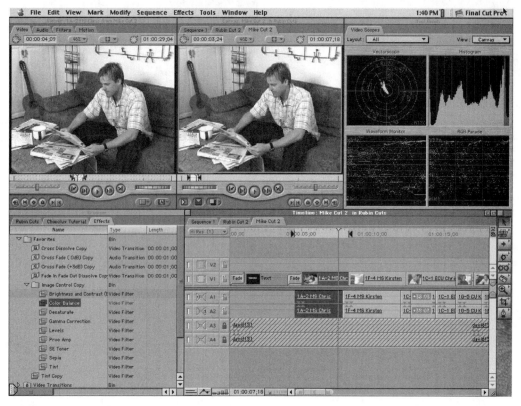

Window > Arrange > Three Up.

Editors who combine editing and effects may want to balance the desire to see more Timeline with smaller (and more) windows on-screen at one time. The windows can be stacked or overlapped. That way, a simple click brings one to the front or sends it to the back, and more windows can be on-screen at once without overcrowding the limited screen real estate.

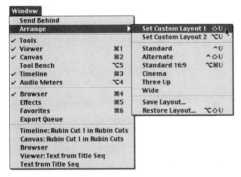

Investigate the FCP-provided preconfigured screen layouts first, but on some afternoon when you have time, experiment with the layout you're most comfortable with. FCP has a convenient way for you to create two custom-configured layouts of your own.

1 Arrange your windows in a way that you really like.

2 Hold down the Option key before you pull down the Windows menu.

3 Select Set Custom Layout 1.

Dean, a long-time nonlinear expert, shows us his preferred FCP display—with Viewer and Canvas set to 50 percent image size, and the Viewer set up wide to accommodate more Timeline detail in the Control tab; the Viewer overlaps the Browser, leaving only about an inch of Browser visible; when the Browser is on top, about an inch of the Viewer is still visible on the right. The Timeline is as wide as the display.

As you can see, you can save two custom window layouts. I recommend you make one for simple editing and, once you've experimented with special effects (later in this chapter) make one for compositing and effects.

Tabs

The innocent little tabs in each window can be far more functional than I have let on. Individual tabs can be separated from the pile of other tabs, pulled free and dragged out to be their very own window. In the Viewer, for instance, the tabs represent "slices" through a selected clip.

If you want to adjust parameters in the Motion tab (which we'll need to do a little later in this lesson), you might want to see what result you're having in picture while you make changes in motion parameters—and the only way to do that is to watch the Video tab at the same time that you adjust the little controls. In the standard stacked-up, tabbed view you have to click back and forth to see what you are doing. There's a simple solution to that problem. In the Viewer click and drag the Video tab away (over the Canvas, let's say), and now you can see what you're doing. Magic: two views of the same material. In most situations, more than two views is probably overkill (but it sure looks cool).

Examine your work in greater detail by pulling the Viewer into more simultaneously accessible tabs. Here, three views are spread across the display at once—Video, Audio, and Motion.

Similarly, if for some reason you want to be messing with a couple of different timelines simultaneously (for instance, if you work by dragging clips from a dailies timeline into your First Cut timeline), drag the tab of one sequence away from the window, and you'll have two timeline windows open at the same time. All tabs share this ability to be dragged away from their originating window and relocated.

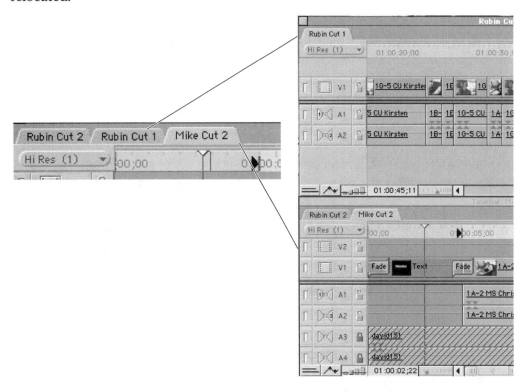

Customizing your interface isn't a one-shot deal; you may continue to refine the way your screen looks as you learn more about editing and take on additional tasks in the post-production process. To change your custom setup, just rearrange the windows the way you want them and reset your Custom Layout.

Adding More Tracks

There are all kinds of reasons you might want to include more tracks in your project. For audio, you might have separate tracks for sound effects and music, where the mix of each needs to be controlled independent of the production tracks and—more importantly—they must all play back simultaneously. Advanced audio editors place dialog from different actors on different tracks, which also aids in mixing the tracks into a cohesive, unified soundtrack.

Today, there is only one important reason to use more tracks: to make different sounds or images occur at the same time in the final sequence. For images, the main reason to add tracks is for executing special effects—mattes, keys, superimpositions, and some titles, for example, are all performed with multiple tracks.

The one important reason for us to use more tracks is simply this: to make different sounds or images mix together and play at the same time in the final sequence. For images, the main reason to add tracks is for executing special effects in composites (sometimes just called *comps*). Mattes, keys, superimpositions, and some titles, for example, are all performed with multiple tracks.

But first a warning: The more tracks in a project, the more time consuming and difficult it is to make any changes to any part of the project. There are many more tracks to keep in sync. There are many more edits that might need adjusting if you make even a small change. Professional film and video editors lock the picture cut before working on all the multiple track stuff—music, effects, and so forth. It's a good rule. With FCP, the way we lock the picture cut is to duplicate that sequence and rename it, as we did with the final version in the last chapter, and then do your effects and compositing in the new sequence. That way, we can always go back to our locked picture cut.

New Sound Tracks for Music

So we'll start simple and build from there.

Open the sequence "Rubin Cut 2." This is my quick pass at the scene from the last chapter, using only the tools and techniques that we've been discussing. I suggest you make a copy of Rubin Cut 2 so you'll have it readily available for comparisons. Rename your copy [Your Name] Cut 2.

The first thing we'll do is add a couple audio tracks. All tracks, regardless of whether for picture or for sound, are added in basically the same way:

1 With the Timeline active, select Sequence > Insert Tracks.

There are shortcuts, but this is a fine start, using the mouse

2 Enter the number of tracks you want to add. I entered "2."

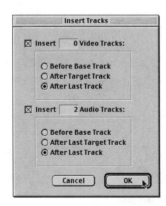

3 You could unclick the check box for Insert __ Video Tracks, but it doesn't matter, as long as the entered amount is 0.

There are three choices for "where" you add the new tracks.

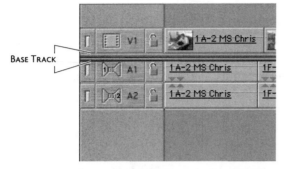

BASE TRACK

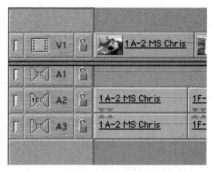

Base tracks are closest to the line that separates video from audio.

Before base track.

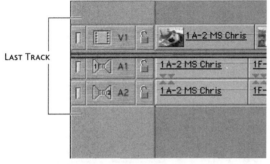

LAST TRACK

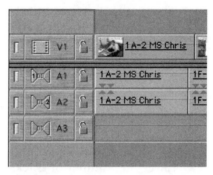

Last tracks are farthest from the baseline, on the outside edges.

After last track.

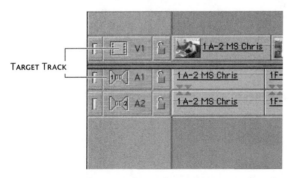

TARGET TRACK

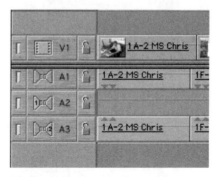

Target tracks can be anywhere you select; in Video there is always only one target possible, in Audio there are two, so FCP is concerned with the "last" target track.

After target track.

4 We want to add the new tracks after the last tracks we currently have, so we'll leave the choices at default.

5 Click OK to confirm your choice and close the dialog box.

Notice that you now have two new, empty audio tracks, A3 and A4, after (actually, underneath) tracks A1 and A2.

Actually, you didn't need to go through that process to add audio tracks. If you're dragging picture or sound directly to the Timeline, FCP knows enough to allow you to add tracks right then and there—no menus, no questions.

Let's get a sound-only clip: in this case, a song called "David (151)." (Written and performed by Suzanne Brewer.) It should be in the Browser.

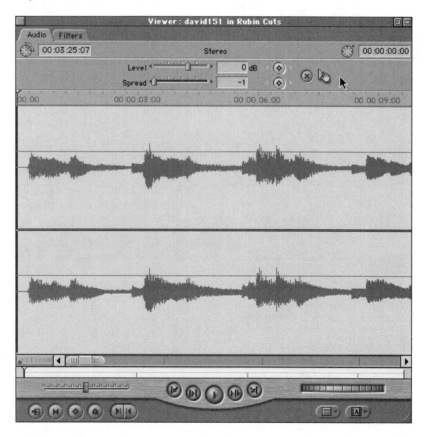

Notice the tabs in the Viewer; since this is a sound-only file, there are only two tabs present: Audio and Filters. There is no "video" or "motion" component to a sound file. Double-click the clip david151 in your Browser, to open it into the Viewer.

You can play a sound file as you would any clip in the Viewer. But you won't be able to drag it to the Canvas (or Timeline) by grabbing anywhere in the window the way you did with a video clip—a source of frustration to beginners. To drag sound files around, use that icon of the hand holding an arrow, located near the top of the window.

When you click that, your cursor becomes a hand and you can treat the sound the way you would any dragable clip. Let's drag it directly down to the Timeline. Watch what happens when you get there—you're making an audio-only overwrite in tracks A3 and A4.

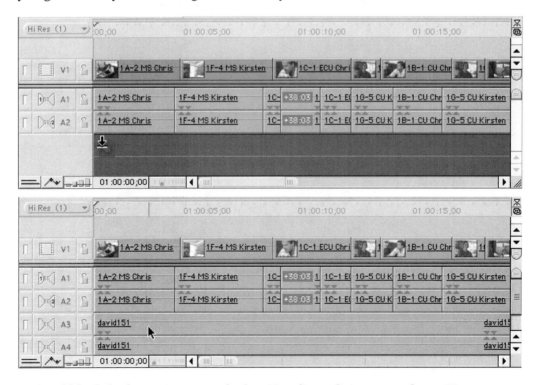

It should look fairly reminiscent of other Timeline editing procedures: You can overwrite your target sound tracks with this clip; you can insert and ripple the existing tracks. But if you drag beneath the existing tracks and drop, you will automatically add tracks for the clip you're moving. Tracks A3 and A4 were added for the stereo music clip.

EXTRA CREDIT: Now that we have a sound track, play the sequence with the production sound tracks muted so you don't hear them (turn the green track lights off); it's a compelling version with just picture and music. If you like, try recutting your picture and production sound so there is no dialog, just a montage of looks and emotions, like a music video. Maybe take out some of the shots where people are talking; maybe use more emotional cut-away shots. I have included a simple example of a Music Video version, labeled Rubin Music Cut.

Go ahead and play the cut in the Timeline with the music added. Interesting. Some of the edits actually work nicely with the music—like you're some kind of genius. That's one of the neat properties of music: It often syncs up with the picture in ways you may never have been able to anticipate or plan.

We're not going to mix this track yet, but since we already covered adjusting audio levels (in Chapter 3), take this opportunity to lower the music volume a little (might I suggest somewhere between -4dB and -8dB, according to your taste), so it doesn't compete with the production tracks.

Lock the music tracks (A3 and A4) while we take a break from music and mess with the picture.

Titles and Text

Titles are essentially another kind of source material that FCP will generate for you. When you were adding slug back in Chapter 3, you might have noticed "Text" was a choice for the video Generator option in the Viewer.

Let's go there now.

Click the Generator button (below the jog wheel in the Viewer) and select Text > Text from the drop-down menu.

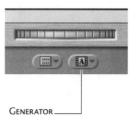

GENERATOR

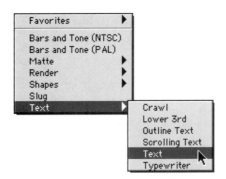

This presents the most basic text option. The Viewer will display a new internally generated source, a "text" source.

The Viewer now has *almost* all the same tabs as it does with a regular clip.

But because this source is picture-only, Audio has been replaced by Controls. The Controls tab contains the primary information about your text clip point.

What has been generated for you is a default clip of text ("SAMPLE TEXT") that is 2 minutes long. In the middle of that 2-minute clip, a 10-second shot has been marked for you (do you see the In and Out marks?). You are now parked at the In.

But this default text isn't even close to the text that you want to add. Select the Controls tab.

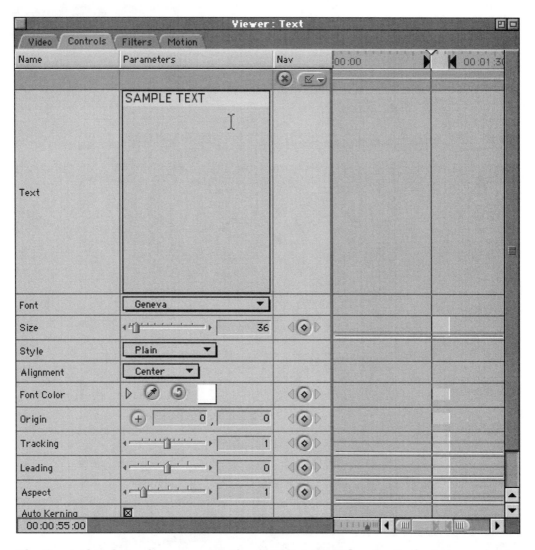

The Controls tab is where you can change what the title says, its font size, color, tracking, and other basic font parameters. Click one of the categories (listed down the left side of the window) to modify it.

First, change the text to read "Chocoluv." Then adjust the font to something sans serif (I used Impact, but any clean headline font will do) and in a significantly larger font size: The default is 36 points, pretty small on most digital displays; try 100.

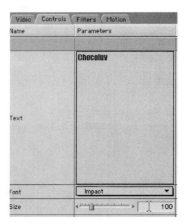

When you go back to the Video tab, you'll see the results of your Controls changes.

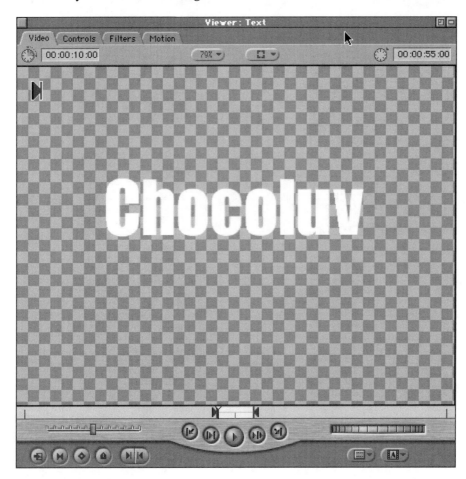

The checkerboard background is a traditional way in graphics applications to indicate that there is *no* background, the title is floating as if on glass. If you place this over video, you'll see the video wherever you now see checkerboard.

Titles are not necessarily effects that require a new video track. Let's look at two ways to treat titles, first as a new track, and second as just another shot added to the existing (single) track of video.

1 Drag this title over to the Timeline and hold it in place just over the clips on V1.

2 Move it back and forth, front to back, and let go when you have the head of it located at about where you want the title to begin. This creates a new track (V2) comprising this text.

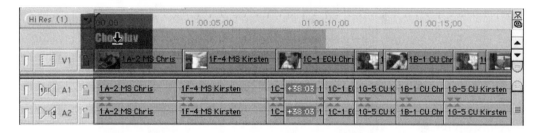

In the Timeline, you'll see this title has been superimposed over the picture track for 10 seconds. Also notice there's a new colored line above the text because this superimposing requires additional processing in order to be previewed. The color of the line depends on whether your system is real-time enabled, and what version of FCP you're using.

Adding Titles to V1

First of all, let's add only a few seconds of this title.

1 Go to the head of the title in the Viewer and press Play; slowly read the title to yourself, and stop when you think it's long enough.

> Sometimes it's tricky to figure out if you're actually "playing" a title. One way you'll know is if the Play icon is highlighted in yellow. Another way is to watch the timecode moving in the window at the top right of the Viewer.

2 Mark a new Out when you feel the time is right. I marked 2 seconds or so. Notice that the marked duration window-top left-shows how long you've made the title.

You also could go to this window and type in your own precise length, and press Return. Titles, in particular, are good places to work with editing using timecode, although we won't go into depth on that in this book.

3 Now, instead of adding a track in V2 (as we did before), target V1 and insert the title before the first shot, as if it were any other clip in the Viewer.

If you see the red bar and need to force FCP to render, select Sequence > Render All.

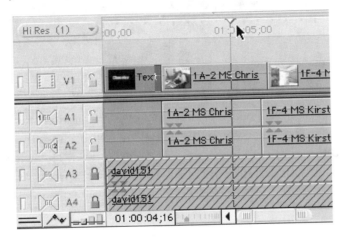

Real Time and Rendered Effects

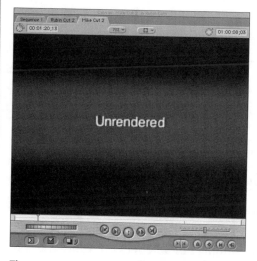

When you add an effect or generator to your Timeline that requires some extra processing by your Mac, the thin render bar at the top of the Timeline turns a different color. If the color is green or yellow, you can play the effect in real time, without rendering. If the color is red, you can still see a single frame previewed in the Canvas when you aren't playing, but you'll need to render this area of the Timeline in order to see the effect play.

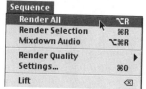

There are two ways to get a shot rendered. You can select the shots and then choose Sequence > Render Selection (if you have In/Out points marked in the Timeline, this option becomes Render IN to OUT). Or you can simply render everything in your sequence by selecting Render All.

Some basic effects in FCP 3 or later can be seen in real time without rendering. The more GHz in your CPU, or the more CPUs you have, the more likely your Mac can show you an effect without rendering.

Play the sequence.

It feels to me like the title is too short. I don't know how long it should be. But I do know that as I hear the music, I *feel* the point where I think the title should end and the picture should start. After I see the title play with the music, it feels more like it needs to be about 5 seconds into the music or so. Play to where you feel the title should end and stop there.

Now that you have parked the playhead where you want something to happen (in this case, where the title should end), get the Ripple Trim tool from the toolbox, select the edit point end of the title, and drag it to the right, to the playhead. When snapping is on, you'll be able to pop it right to the playhead, where you want the shot to end. All the other shots (in picture and sound together) ripple down to make room.

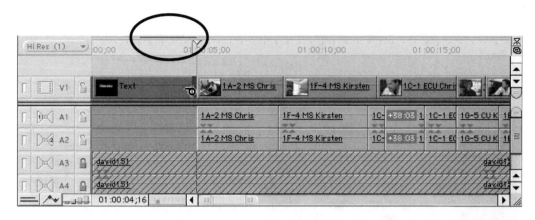

The part of this title that was rendered before is still rendered, but the new length is not: Notice the colored bar over only the added part of the title.

As you can see, a title is pretty much like any other clip, even when edited into a sequence. The difference is that, like many effects, a title must be rendered to appear. But a title over black is one of the simplest of all effects to render, so on any Mac it's liable to be a short wait.

Adding Titles Using New Picture Tracks

Adding basic titles can generally be done in the base video track (V1). But on occasion you will want titles that overlap with pictures, and to do that we will need to add new picture tracks.

Let's create a new title card. This one is going to be a sort of MTV-style label, in the lower third of the frame, on the left:

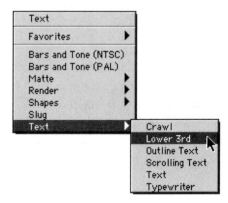

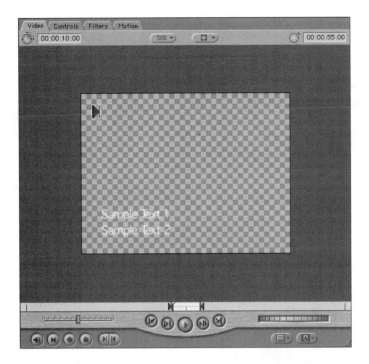

More important than the Viewer's Video tab for text generators is the Controls tab. Click it to adjust the material in the two text boxes. Let's enter something in each:

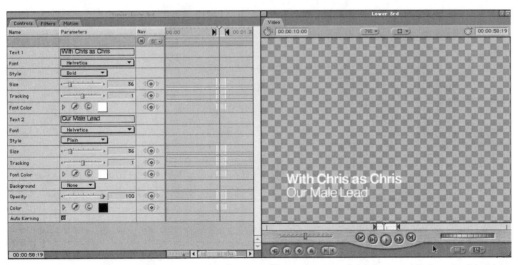

I pulled the Video tab away from the Controls tab so I could see what I am doing better while I work with titles.

I made the top text bold and the bottom not bold, but they're the same Helvetica font. I will drag the Video tab to the right side of the screen so we can see the Controls tab and the Video at the same time.

1   Using the Mark Out button on the Viewer, I shorten the title to approximately 3 seconds.

2   In the Timeline, play and stop at what feels to you like a good spot for the lower-third text to start.

3   With the playhead exactly where you want the title to begin, drag the title down to the Timeline until it snaps to the playhead.

4   Drop the title *above* the V1 track. Notice that a new video track (V2) is added, and the title is in it.

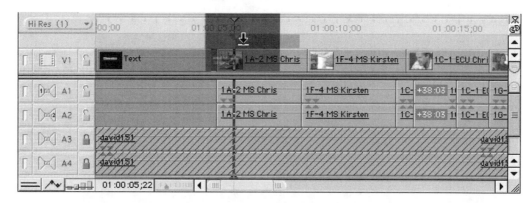

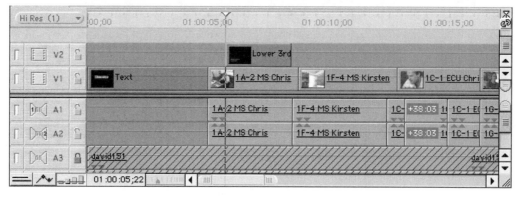

It looked fine in the Viewer; it appears fine in the Timeline, but now that I see it in the Canvas, with the background material, the title in small white letters is hard to read over the video. You're not stuck—you could make the font bolder or the type larger, but I have another suggestion. You'll need to go to a different tab to fix it.

Adding a Drop Shadow

Here's our first fairly significant departure from the "way things tend to work." I said in Chapter 1 that the only way to get something in the Viewer is by selecting it in the Browser. The edits appear only on the Canvas. But there's an exception to these general rules: You can double-click a clip in the Timeline to load it into the Viewer. When you do this, you are effectively taking a shot from the finished sequence and putting it up in a workspace where you can adjust it—in the Viewer.

A shot brought to the Viewer from the Timeline is not much different from clips taken from the Browser, except that changes made here are incorporated into the sequence in the Timeline right away. It's as if you were adjusting shots in the Timeline itself, even though you're working on them in the Viewer space. The big advantage is that when you're done working on them, you don't have to save the adjustments, or put them back in the Timeline; they just *are*.

Let's double-click the title effect we just created in V2. It's selected in the Timeline and it appears in the Viewer.

While this title looks very similar to the raw title before it was cut into the sequence, it isn't the same. It's now composited over picture, so it looks different. Not so good. Click the Controls tab and let's adjust it.

Now click the Motion tab.

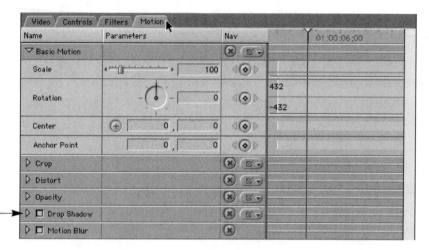

A number of physical attributes of the frames you're looking at can be modified here—the size of the frame, its rotation, crop, distortion, opacity, and motion blur. The odd one here, for me, is Drop Shadow, which doesn't seem like a frame attribute so much as a text attribute. Still, if you're going to do text or titles of any kind, it's critical to know where Drop Shadow is and how to use it. I believe that all titles in video need a drop shadow. It can be subtle, but it increases the legibility of text on-screen, in particular when there is competing visual information in the form of a moving video background.

If you click the check box by Drop Shadow, you'll see the default setting for this effect appear on the Canvas. (You want to see it in the Canvas and not on the Video tab of the effect, because to make these kinds of judgments about an effect you'll likely want to see it in the context of the other video in the sequence.)

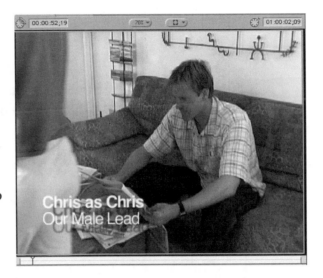

If you don't like the default (and I don't), open up the Drop Shadow feature by clicking the triangle, and reveal a small window of the Drop Shadow parameters.

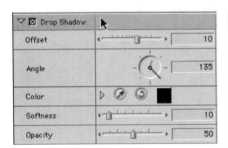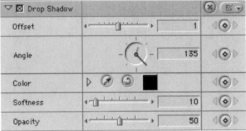

The one we're going for is Offset; its default is 10, but let's change it to 1. Depending on how busy the background image is and the size of the title (among other factors), a subtle drop shadow offset runs in the range of 1 to 4. Set higher than 4, the shadow loses the ability to help the main text stand out from the background.

When you're done experimenting with your drop shadow, you'll notice the red bar is now back in the Timeline. Because you changed a parameter on an already-rendered effect, you need to render the effects again. After you review the effect, if the title feels too long or too short, you can easily trim its length with a trim or the Razor Blade tool.

Title Location: Control > Origin vs. Motion > Center

Moving the location of a title on the screen can dramatically impact how a title feels to a viewer. Main titles are created in the center of the display by default—which makes some sense, but defies the aesthetic rule of thirds which aids in good screen design. To move the text you have two options.

Under the Controls tab, you can click the "+" next to Origin. This resets where FCP places a title with respect to the video frame. The default origin is in the center of the text box (0,0 in X,Y coordinates). When you click the + you will see the origin in the window, and if you click elsewhere in the frame, the origin (and thus the title) will move accordingly. This is the most appropriate method of moving a title around.

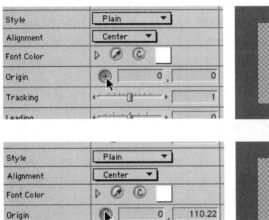

The alternative doesn't move the title per se, but moves the entire frame. Under the Motion tab, you can scale and move the frame—which of course moves and scales the title. Center in the Motion tab works the same way as Origin in the Controls tab. The results may look the same, but the method is profoundly different.

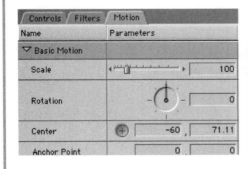

Basic Transition Effects

A transition effect is a modification to the way one shot ends and the next begins. Even though a transition effect in FCP is technically just an effect that is dropped over what is traditionally called a "transition," in FCP the more accurate term "transition effect" is generally shortened to "transition." (When I mean transition effect, however, I'll call it that, to fully differentiate it from ordinary edit points. A sequence without transition effects is called "cuts-only." There are many variations on how transition effects are placed on a splice (Start On, Center On, and End On Edit) and ample customizations are possible, but we're going to focus exclusively on the FCP defaults for transition effects.

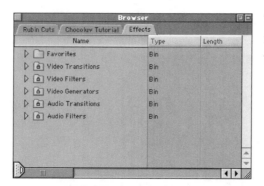

Transition effects are maintained in a folder in the Browser, under the Effects tab.

Open the Video Transitions folder, then the Dissolves folder, to reveal an assortment of options. We're going to examine two of them.

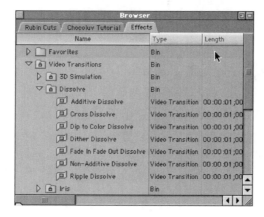

Fade In Fade Out Dissolve

Fades are a sophisticated way to ease into and out of titles and opening/closing shots of video. Fades create a feeling of *closure*. Most commercials sport a 10-frame (fast!) fade at the head and tail. Many television shows start and end each act with a fade.

A fade *out* will gradually darken a shot to black, usually over the course of a few seconds or less. A fade *in* does the reverse. Fades centered on transitions don't lengthen shots; they take whatever shot is cut into a sequence and, starting at the splice point, build their duration from there.

In FCP, two fades are built back-to-back, as a sort of convenient option if you are using fades in the middle 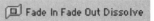 of a program. This Fade In Fade Out Dissolve, like many special effects in FCP, is represented as an icon you can drag and drop. You drag the dissolve from the Effects menu in the Browser and drop it over a splice in the Timeline.

For shots like the first or last in a sequence, that seem to have no splice, place the transition at the beginning or end (respectively) of the shot.

Drag the Fade In Fade Out to the first shot in the sequence, the Chocoluv title. Place it over the head of the title and let go.

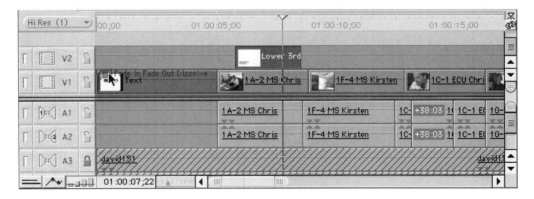

We are going to stay with the 1-second default of the fade in/out (half a second—or 15 frames—on each side of the fade). Let's add three more of these dissolves.

The first, we'll add to the end of the title and beginning of the first video shot. This time we want to fade out the title, and then fade in the next shot, so we want to drop the effect directly over the edit point—it should look evenly distributed over the transition:

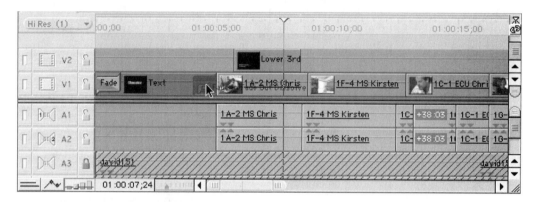

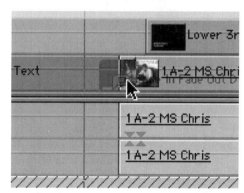

Now the simple title card fades in and out, and the first shot of the program fades in. A last nicety is to fade in and out the lower-third title.

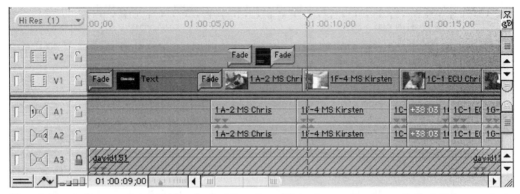

These fades are close to other transitions in the V1 track, and if they're too close (or particularly if they overlap) they may look clunky, like a mistake. It's generally good to keep transition effects away from other transitions; if the material doesn't allow that to happen, just be sure to watch the results carefully.

Fades effectively shorten a shot, so an almost-too-short shot will feel shorter if you've applied a fade in/out to it. Plan the length of titles accordingly.

Cross Dissolve

The next most basic transition effect is popularly called a "dissolve," but is technically referred to as a "cross dissolve"—an effect pretty familiar to most people, where the A-side fades out at the same time as the B-side fades in. A "center-point dissolve" is one in which, at the location of the edit—the midpoint of the transition—you see an image that's 50 percent shot A and 50 percent shot B.

Unlike a fade, where there is no overlapping of images in the A and B sides, a dissolve replaces one picture with another. Where a fade provides some sense of closure, a dissolve moves you forward. But most importantly, because the two shots in a dissolve can be seen onscreen at the same time, the content of those frames needs to be considered—how they look superimposed.

Even though I often use fades, I hardly ever use dissolves. Perhaps because they are overused, or misused, by beginners. Dissolves have many fine uses (including the depiction of time passing gently along between shots), but these uses hardly ever include transitions within a scene, particularly one in which a conversation is taking place. Still, dissolves are handy and merit a little examination.

How to Add a Transition

A dissolve or any transition effect requires video material that is not present in the Timeline in the cuts-only version of a sequence. When you add a cross dissolve, for instance, FCP must extend the video of both shots being shown so it can slowly switch (that is, *dissolve*) from one to the other

Below are two shots cut together as a simple splice.

To create the centered dissolve, both shots must be extended by the same amount. A 1-second dissolve adds 15 frames to the tail of the A-side and 15 frames to the head of the B-side. Thus, to FCP a cross dissolve looks like this:

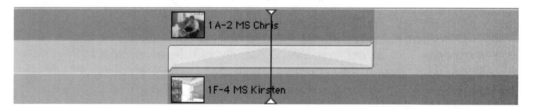

If you look closely at the figure above, you'll see the dark-shaded area in the top track that represents the 15 frames added to the tail of the A-side, or outgoing clip. And in the lower track, there's a similar dark-shaded area representing the 15 frames added to the head of the B-side, or incoming clip.

Now here's the tricky part, where many beginners get frustrated. There are times when you want to make a dissolve and FCP prevents it because it sees there isn't enough material in your underlying source clip to execute the effect. If, for instance, the B-shot's In-point started only 10 frames into a clip, then it would be impossible to add 15 frames to the head—there's not enough material. That's why FCP (mysteriously sometimes) won't let you add a transition effect.

Another tricky thing about adding any transition effect (including dissolves): Even if FCP doesn't warn you, there may be an aesthetic problem. The 15 frames added for you may be new material you haven't previewed yet that will look bad when included in the dissolve and mixed with the other shot. Maybe it's a slate, maybe it's another character or scene. (These are sometimes called "flash frames," because they often produce a little flash or bump in the transition.) Whatever the reason, when you perform a dissolve, you always want to review the result closely see how it looks.

Let's add one dissolve to this sequence, between the shot of Kirsten standing watching Chris and the one of Chris looking up. (It's about the only reasonable spot for a dissolve, as it could give the feeling that she's been standing here a bit. Though it's a stretch.)

1 Drag the Cross Dissolve icon from the Effects tab of the Browser and drop it when it's centered on the transition.

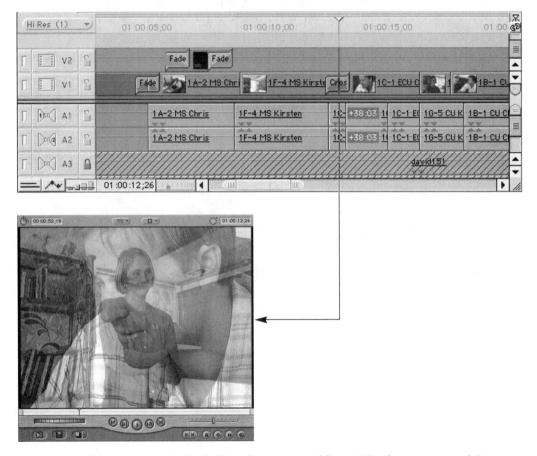

This creates a default dissolve 1 second long. That's not unusual for a dissolve, but you might want it to last longer.

2 Double-click the dissolve icon in the Timeline to open it in the Viewer.

You can adjust many of the subtle features of this dissolve in the Viewer.

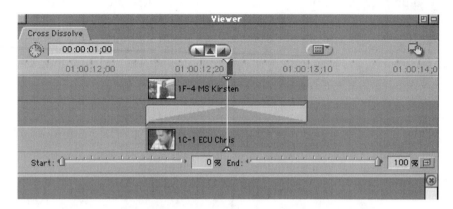

3 Enter a new duration in the timecode-duration window at the top left. It now says "01;00" or 1 second; change this to 02;00.

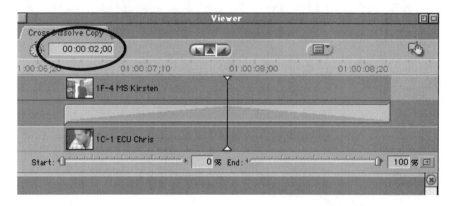

The icon of the dissolve in the Timeline also changes when you lengthen the effect to accurately represent the time covered by the transition.

It's all right, I guess. You can keep it or delete it, as you like.

To delete it, just select the dissolve in the Timeline and press Delete. The transition will be restored to a cut.

Other Transitions

There are other transition effects you can test out, too. A "wipe" transitions from an A-shot to a B-shot using some kind of geometric pattern. There are a myriad of possibilities in the custom wipe department. At some point, in your spare time, I suggest trying out the five other transition effects included in FCP 3.

- An **Additive Dissolve** is like a cross-dissolve, but the brightness of the images is added together instead of averaged out. It can look like a fade in/out to white instead of black.

- A **Dip to Color Dissolve** is like a fade out/fade in, but rather than fading to black, you can select the color you'd like to dissolve in and out of (the color you see full on at the midpoint of the transition).

- A **Dither Dissolve** is an interesting transition that breaks an image into a noise pattern and then back to an image. It's fancy, more trendy, and therefore easily overused.

- A **Non-Additive Dissolve** is like an additive dissolve, but the images do not *add*, and thus produce a dissolve through black but with a slightly different visual effect. (No point trying to describe it in words—try it if you're curious.)

- A **Ripple Dissolve** is the most like traditional wipes. This transition looks like a pond ripple (made by dipping your finger in a pool of water) and is slower to render because it takes a bit more processing than most other transitions. (Don't confuse this effect's "ripple" with the editing concept *rippling*. They have nothing to do with each other.)

Keyframes

You know that video plays at 30 frames per second. If you wanted to draw 30 pictures, and play them one after another, you could create a little 1-second animation. Think about how long it takes to draw 30 pictures. Now think about how long it would take to draw a full-length movie.

One of the things that came out of early advances in animation is the idea that when you are animating something or someone, you don't really need to draw all 30 frames. Not initially. What is most important are key moments in the character's motion. For instance, a moving hand starts in one spot, and after a few seconds, you want it to be in another.

Eventually all the frames between these two moments must be drawn, but when you're working out the animation in the first place, you need only begin with the most important, "key" frames.

Thus, the art of animating—whether a computer-generated character, a flying logo, or a hand-drawn animal—begins with first establishing the key frames or *keyframes*. Then later, you go back and do the laborious drawings between them—called *inbetweening* (or *tweening* in some software).

Why am I telling you this? Because if you want any reasonable control of titles and motion effects in FCP (or any other software that is billed as an animation tool), you must fully comprehend this idea of setting keyframes and then letting the computer do the inbetweening.

In FCP there is a button that adds a keyframe. It looks like this:

At any keyframe, you can set every parameter FCP offers to modify a shot—the color correction, the size of the frame, the opacity, the position of the frame on the screen, and more. The list is long. The power of effects is in keyframes.

Keyframes are primarily added in the Viewer, under the tabs for Filters and Motion. This is not the only place where you can use keyframes, but it's a good place to start.

In your working sequence, double-click the opening title card, Chocoluv, to open it in the Viewer.

Look closely at the Controls, Filters, and Motion tabs for this shot. They all have four columns: Name, Parameters, Nav, and...that last one has no name, but it should look familiar. It's a little timeline, related to the big scale in the Timeline window.

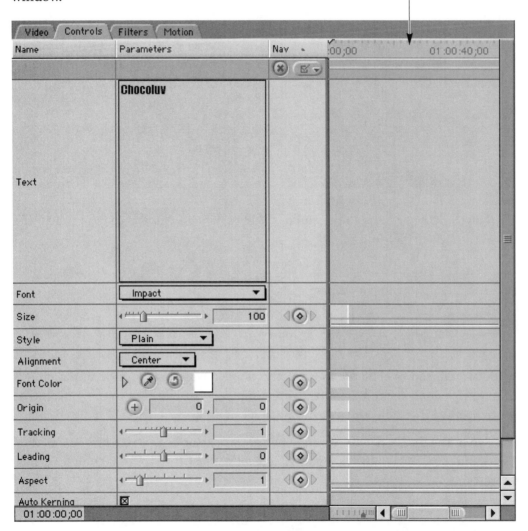

This fourth column is where you place keyframes. In FCP, this column is called the Keyframe Graph. You'll see that in the Nav column there are many attributes of this text that present a keyframe button. Let's say we want to animate the title text, making it start large and then shrink. We need to set at least two key frames: its size at the start of the shot and its size at the end. FCP will do your inbetweening.

You must begin by indicating where the first keyframe should go. You do that by actually moving the playhead to the location where you want the action to start. You can move there using the Canvas scrubber, the Timeline playhead, the Viewer video scubber, or the Keyframe Graph playhead. I like to use the main Timeline playhead.

Here we are at the head of the shot, which also happens to be the head of the Fade In. Let's press the Keyframe button in the Size row. (It can be a little hard to see when it's right at the beginning of a sequence, but you can see it there if you look closely.)

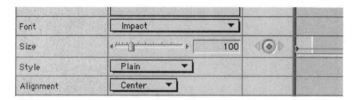

We'll also add a keyframe to the end of the shot, which happens to fall in the middle of the fade in/fade out.

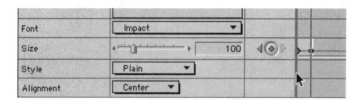

With two keyframes here, the Viewer gives you a navigational option of popping from keyframe to keyframe. Use the directional arrows adjacent to the button that move headward or tailward, a keyframe at a time.

If we go to the first keyframe, we can change the size or leave it; it's now 100 points. That's fine. Pop to the other keyframe; here let's adjust the size to 30 points, which is pretty small.

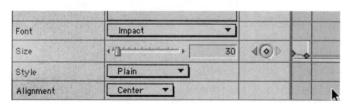

This is a simple two-keyframe animation, The title starts big and over the course of the shot shrinks until it ultimately fades out.

Render it and take a look.

There are so many permutations of the FCP parameters and effects that entire books have been written about applying these and other third-party effects (like Adobe's After Effects and Boris Effects, to name two) in FCP.

Compositing: What It Is, and Why We Aren't Doing It Here

This is not a book on compositing. But I do think it's important to understand some of the basic ideas of compositing and how FCP will address them.

Compositing is the art of stacking up layers of video and making them look good in the process. When you stack up video, you have to imagine they are piled up on a light table and you are watching them from the top down.

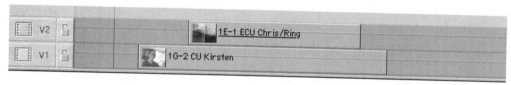

If a layer is opaque (opacity = 100 percent) then you're not going to be able to see anything underneath it. If a layer is translucent (opacity = 0 percent) then it will be a clear window, and you won't see any of images in the layer itself. Let's call this layer opacity Principle Number One.

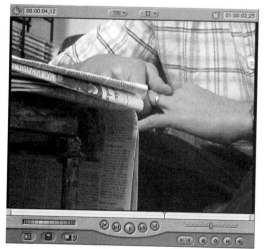

Here's layer one over layer two. Not much to see on the left, where layer one is 100 percent opaque. On the right its opacity is 30 percent and you can see layer two underneath.

But video in a layer doesn't always need to be full screen. The video can be shrunk to fill only a portion of the screen. If you did this, you'd have a kind of "window-in-a-window" or picture-in-picture feature, where you could watch two independent moving pictures (sometimes called *video streams*) at the same time. Let's call resizing video and moving the little box on the screen Principle Number Two.

Now both layers have 100 percent opacity, but layer one (the top layer) has been reduced to 30 percent of its former size. On the left, the upper image is in the default position, centered; on the right I have moved it (Motion tab > Center) to the lower-right corner.

But if that were all that compositing could do, it wouldn't be all that interesting. You've been working with video images that are full screen in a rectangular format that has an aspect ratio of 4:3. But there are tools that will allow you to cut out parts of an image. It's this cutting out bits and pieces of images and compositing them together into a new whole image that's interesting, and produces most of the impressive power of image compositing. Let's call the special ability to cut out pieces of an image (using keys and mattes) Principle Number Three.

Here the upper image has been filtered with a color key, so you can see through only the parts of it that have the chosen range of color.

By cutting out video, repositioning and resizing the bits over other video, you begin to sense the nature of video compositing. There is much more to this, but hopefully this short introduction will allow you to see how these often-complex effects integrate into FCP.

Filter Effects

A Filter effect "processes" a selected shot, changing the way the image on the screen looks by changing (à la Photoshop) the pixels in each frame of video. Filters can blur and sharpen shots, adjust color and noise, or even give the video a "film-look." Filter effects, like motion effects, generally take more processing power and time than basic transition effects and titles. To make matters worse, filters can be added to shots that already have filters, and as they stack up, the rendering time can expand dishearteningly. Some of this problem can be mediated by setting up FCP to render with lower-quality video, but that is beyond the purview of this book.

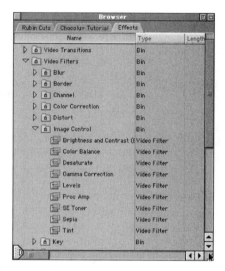

I'd like to present a very plain filter effect just so you can see one in action. It's one I use often: Tint.

Basically, Tint makes a color image into black-and-white (technically called "grayscale," because it has many shades of gray) and then adds a single-color tint on top of the gray. (And believe me: There are a handful of ways to create this result using different filters or color-correction tools.)

Sometimes poor video production value is due to bad lighting, bad color temperatures (yielding odd colors), or mismatched colors between shots. Also, it is the color part of a video signal (called *chrominance*) that reveals poorer-quality camera technology and image compression. The black-and-white part of the video signal (called *luminance*) will be of higher quality than the chrominance. In many cases, lose the color, and pick up the image quality.

Drop the tint effect onto a shot in your Timeline, and "poof," it looks like a black-and-white movie because the default tint color in this effect is "no color."

Double-click that shot and it appears in the Viewer. Look in the Filters tab and you'll see where the Tint filter has landed. If you want to see what the default parameters of this filter are, you can check them here. If you want to change those settings, you also do that here. Tint is nice and simple, with only two parameters (color and amount).

You've dropped this filter on the first shot in the sequence. About a 4-second shot. Select Render All.

Tint works the same way all filter effects work; it is applied to a shot and has parameters associated with it that can be accessed in the Filter tab and animated with keyframes in the associated Viewer timeline.

Modifying the Filter with Keyframes

If the filter is to be evenly applied to the entire shot, we're done. But often you want to animate an effect, even a filter effect.

Using the Cue to Head button on the screen, move the playhead to the first frame of this black-and-white shot.

In the Viewer, click the Keyframe button in the Amount row.

Then in the Canvas, cue to the last frame of *picture* in this shot. (Watch out: The sound ends before the picture does!)

FCP estimated this 4-second shot would take about 2 minutes (120 seconds) to render. That's a ratio of 30:1 or 30X out of real time on a 400 MHz G3 laptop, running FCP 3 in OS 9.2.2. Compare that to the same shot on a dual GHz G4 running FCP 3 in OS 10.1, where the same effect renders in 8 seconds, a ratio of 2:1 or 2X real time. Good thing we weren't trying to render the entire 50-second video sequence!

Mark a keyframe here, too, in the Viewer, and change the amount of the Tint to 0. What we've told FCP to do is to ramp the tint up in this shot, beginning in black-and-white and ending in color. The timeline will draw a line between these points and show the ramp of tint that will occur during this shot. You can click around on various frames in the Timeline window to preview the effect.

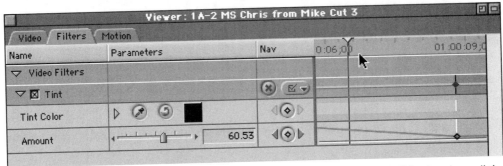

We ramp the tint in this first shot, from black-and-white (right after the title), slowly building in color until the end, when it's fully in color and cuts to the next shot.

Since we're modifying a shot that is already cut into the sequence, all we need to do to see the animated filter is to render.

Video Favorites

Any effect that you use frequently can be dragged from the Effects folder (or from a sequence) into the Video Favorites folder. A copy is created there so you can conveniently store your frequently used (or custom-modifed) effects.

I keep five basic effects here. I find this small number of favorites handles many of my editing effects needs, but of course you may add your own favorites as you work.

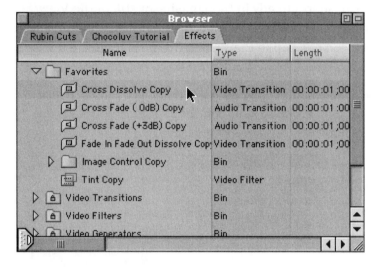

- Cross Dissolve
- Fade In Fade Out Dissolve
- Image Control (the whole folder, but particularly Tint)
- Cross Fade (+3dB)
- Cross Fade (0dB)

Basic Speed Effects

Speed Effects are rendered effects where the playing direction and speed of a shot can be modified. Speed effects are useful when, due to some problem in production (camera operator impatience, for instance), a shot you want to use is too short. If you only have 25 good frames of a shot that you think should run about 1.5 seconds, slowing the good frames down can make an acceptable shot out of what would otherwise be garbage.

You can apply speed effects to shots already in the Timeline or still in the Viewer. Because speed effects must be rendered before you can see how they look, I don't recommend changing the speed of a clip in the Viewer. But once it's just a few seconds long, as cut into the sequence, it's fair game for necessary adjustments.

Let's say we want to make Chris's stunned reaction a little longer, but there just isn't enough material on the source side to lengthen the shot in traditional ways using trim.

1 In the Timeline, select the shot you think is too fast (or too slow—although this is a comical effect that only works once in a while).

2 Choose Modify > Speed.

This will bring up the Speed submenu, where you can select the amount of the modification and a few other interesting aspects of motion effects.

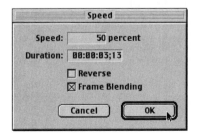

Changing the speed of a shot to 50 percent will make it slow down by half and therefore take twice as long to play. That's a significant speed change.

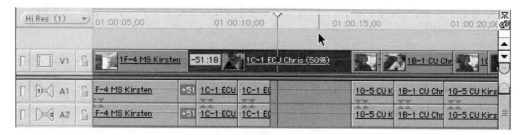

Slowing it down by half makes it a little long, and you'll see when you render and play it that it looks visibly different from the other shots. Only small changes in speed will go unnoticed by viewers (assuming that's what you want.)

1 Select Undo.

2 Choose Modify > Speed again, but this time only change the shot to 80 percent speed.

3 Turn off Frame Blending, which is useful only for speeds of about 40 percent or less.

4 Render again.

This is a far less noticeable adjustment, and sometimes it's your only option when you're working to wrest a particular feeling from the uncooperative source material.

By the way, if you perform a speed effect on both picture and sound, the sound will be augmented as well, often with undesirable results. The alternative is to adjust picture alone. However, this will create a gap in the sound track. This can be filled with slug, but it's better either to do a rolling trim of the sound or to insert some ambient sound, perhaps the same (quiet) sound in the tracks used just before the gap (sometimes called "stealing audio").

Putting Them Together: A Title Sequence

A project's title is sometimes more complex than the editing of the project itself. It can be simple, yes, but if you want to try special effects and filters, creating a title sequence is a safe harbor, limited to a short format (5–15 seconds probably). And while the titles can easily be incorporated into the edit of the main sequence itself (as we did earlier), it's often more efficient to separate them since they are built in such different ways.

I do the following for a down-and-dirty, all-purpose opening when I have no time to mess around but I'd like something sort of distinct.

1 Pick a shot (pretty much any shot).

2 Blur it, by going to the Effects tab and choosing Video Filters > Blur > Gaussian Blur > 20 pixels. (When you start getting more advanced, try other modifications to this background image from the Video Filters selections.)

3 Make a title card, with large, bold, white letters, and a 3-pixel offset drop shadow.

4 Take a short riff of music.

5 Stack the elements up as follows: music (A1, A2), blurred background video (V1), title card (V2). The music should be longest, then the background, then the title.

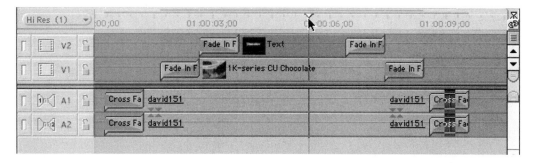

They should stack up like a little pyramid, so that the order of events is as follows:

Fade in music; music plays; fade in background; a moment later, fade in title and hold it long enough to read twice, slowly; then fade out title; fade out background; and, a moment later, fade out music.

As your desire for complexity grows, you might try to animate the titles—for example, how they arrive onto and exit the screen. You could use different effects on the background, maybe in combination, and maybe with different levels of animation over the course of the video. And finally, experiment with the music; it can be a montage, fading in and out combinations of production sound and music. You'll start to see why you might want to keep this project self-contained in its own Sequence rather than building it on top of your edited master.

Although fundamental editing concepts and tools can be described in a chapter or two, this chapter barely touches on the kinds of "fancy" things you can do once you lock in your basic story structure. Remember, though, that effects tend to make every part of post-production slow down, due to the complexity you've added in terms of more tracks (keeping them in sync, knowing what's there), and the rendering and re-rendering of composited materials, filters, and animated changes to shots. This chapter introduced you to the effects an editor is most likely to need day to day. You now have the foundation for exploring the power that FCP affords.

CHAPTER 5 # Be Your Own Assistant

No question about it, editing is the fun part. And Final Cut Pro makes it pretty enjoyable. But there are many aspects of post-production work that are not quite as exciting: setting up equipment; dealing with technological problems; logging, capturing, and organizing materials; and outputting videotape dubs or DVDs for distribution. Many of these tasks are repetitive, non-creative, and time-consuming.

If you're like me, you probably don't have an assistant to do all the geeky technical and laborious work. But it has to get done. So you'll need to be your own assistant.

The Assistant's Job

There is a great tradition in Hollywood for how people become editors: You begin as an apprentice to a professional editor. You fetch the coffee and you get to see the editor work once in awhile. Then after some time, you might become an assistant editor. Assistants do all the grunt work, including supervising much of the post-production. The editor, on the other hand, is the creative master of the project—makes the aesthetic decisions, generally handles the editing system, works with the director and/or producers, and of course, makes the big bucks. An editor and an assistant are a dynamic team.

Which brings us to you.

This chapter is not going to teach you to be a professional assistant editor, a skillful organizer of paying projects. I'm assuming that if you're assisting yourself, you hope to spend as little time doing assistant work as possible and would rather focus on the editing. I am also assuming that you're using FCP for personal video projects, maybe for fun, and only want to learn enough to get by, to start editing. So we're going to investigate the kind of assisting you need if you're making what I call "video sketches," short personal videos (discussed in detail in *The Little Digital Video Book*). The past few chapters have been for editors, about editing. Now you'll need to learn a little about being your own best assistant.

Your job will be

- to organize your clips efficiently
- to capture video quickly
- to understand key principles of video and Macintosh technology
- to output your final (or intermediate) cut sequences to digital tape
- to prepare your final cuts for burning to DVD

Personal Video Management

Your first job as an assistant is to manage the post-production process. What that consists of, and how difficult a project is to organize, depends largely on the project. The *amount* of material shot for a project is one factor to consider: More material probably means greater need for pre-organization. The *style* of production is the other factor: It determines how the shots themselves will be labeled and retrieved.

Decisions about labeling and organization are best made before any editing begins. This organizational phase of the project can take a great deal of time, and how much time you spend should be weighed against the total time allotted for post-production. For personal projects, I want to spend as little time organizing as possible.

Organizational decisions made early on, like editing resolution and how much hard disk space you need, have an impact down the line on how long your project takes to complete. For example, although keeping timecode unbroken is a production task, the results of the work are only felt in post-production. You must also consider the trade-off between how long it takes to find video you're looking for (much easier with well-organized tapes) versus how long it takes to label and describe all the shots.

Shot Labels

Naming tapes is critical, if you don't want to lose material in piles of tapes. The style of your production largely determines how you label clips. When you shoot your videos, there are two paths you can take: *scripted* and *unscripted*.

Unscripted projects are shot in a documentary style. They have little or no planning (no scripts, no storyboards), little or no production tools (no tripods, boom microphone operators, or light kits), and probably no actors. There are no slates, no scene names, and there is no obvious way to label and organize the projects. In these cases, clips can be organized by date shot (for example, 04-15-02 morning) or simply by serialized numbers (such as shot 01), which represent entire tapes or large parts of tapes.

Scripted projects, even the amateur scene we've been working on, must be highly organized before the shoot. They involve some degree of pre-production, shot planning (maybe storyboarding), and on- and off-camera talent. For these projects, the editor's connection to the shoot is often through the script, lined with notes from production. Scripted material must be logged and broken down into individual takes (again, as was done for the Chocoluv Tutorial) and organized some way in FCP and on the Macintosh so the editor can easily find and access each shot as needed based on scene and take numbers.

The tradition is to name clips with a scene number followed by the take number, separated by a hyphen (or occasionally a period or underscore). Thus, Scene 1, Take 5 is "1-5."

Managing Disk Space

As an assistant, the first thing you may want to consider in organizing is the amount of source material compared to the hard disk space available on the editing system. To have a "proper" nonlinear editing experience you want to have enough room on your computer to fit *all* the source material.

If all the video can't fit, you have two options. Either do a pre-edit and selectively capture material (a sort of linear edit before the nonlinear edit) or use FCP 3's offline resolution feature, which lets you trade high-quality DV resolution (at 4.5 minutes per GB) for sub-VHS-quality Photo JPEG resolution (at 45 minutes per GB). Working at lower resolutions is fine for making most edit decisions, but when you're finished editing you will likely want to take the additional step of re-capturing your final cut in a higher resolution. If you logged your material correctly (using accurate reel numbers and unbroken timecode) re-capturing is easy and semi-automated, although it is time-consuming.

If you want a project to be simple—and I always do—avoid the offline/online resolution thing entirely and only work at DV resolution. This requires that you have enough hard disk space to hold all the source material for your video.

File Organization

File organization is the hardest thing to do when you're just starting out. I mean, why come up with a filing system or numbering paradigm when you've only got three digital cassettes and this is your first project? On the other hand, you can start with good habits early on or later you can wish you had. If you put it off, you'll eventually cross the line: You'll have too many unlabeled tapes to deal with and "capture scratch" files in untitled folders all over your hard disks. At that point, you just have to go forward with some intelligence and forethought. When that day comes, here are some things you'll wish you'd known.

Videotape Reel Names

Cassette tapes are also called "reels" and a tape name is comparable to a reel number. If you do nothing else organizationally, all your videotapes should be uniquely labeled and numbered.

I use this simple naming system: All my tapes are designated as either "S" for source material shot in the digital format; "M" for master material (the output videos of FCP); or "A" for analog material I have dubbed into the digital format for source material.

Once I give a tape a letter, then I just append a sequential number to it, starting at 001. For example, the videotape I shot for the Chocoluv Tutorial was S070. Three-digit numbers will make for years of videotapes.

There is a strong inclination to name tapes with text labels ("Summer Vacation") or a date (6-2002). While FCP can handle a range of text reel names, I find it hard to locate tapes if they are not put away, and I never know how to put away tapes with names or dates. I can't easily tell if

I am missing one. So when I do use text or dates, it is always in addition to a basic reel number.

Once a tape has a reel name, I can use it in FCP, I can log it on a logsheet, and I can put it on a shelf to use later, at my convenience.

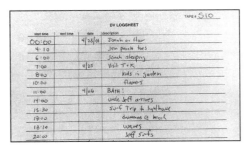

A logsheet

My log book

Media Files vs. Data Files

Digital video makes for large computer files—as we've mentioned, 1 GB of hard disk space holds less than 5 minutes of video. When digital video (and digital audio, for that matter) is stored on a computer, the file is known as a "media file." But media files alone are not functional units for editing.

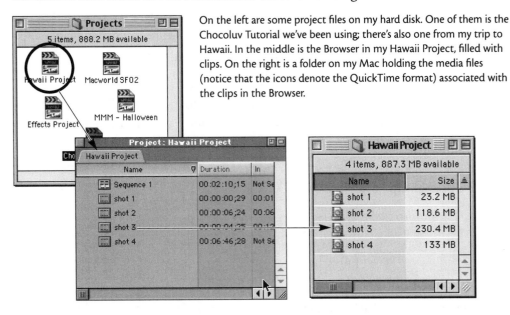

On the left are some project files on my hard disk. One of them is the Chocoluv Tutorial we've been using; there's also one from my trip to Hawaii. In the middle is the Browser in my Hawaii Project, filled with clips. On the right is a folder on my Mac holding the media files (notice that the icons denote the QuickTime format) associated with the clips in the Browser.

When FCP creates a new project, the project is a repository of all kinds of data (sometimes called "metadata") about media files. But a project is not a media file. Neither is a clip or a sequence. A clip (the object in FCP that most resembles a media file) is a tiny little data file that is *linked* to a media file.

FCP data files, often just called "project files," are relatively small. All the data (the FCP project file) for my recent 15-minute annual retrospective video was only 350 KB—though the associated media files nearly filled a 40 GB hard disk.

A clip can exist without a media file connected. When a media file and a clip lose their link, the clip will remain in the Browser with a red line through it—it's then called an "offline clip."

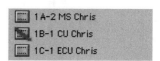

A clip with a red line through it is "offline"—as in "not connected to a network" and should not to be confused with *offline resolution*, which is a completely different thing.

A clip could be disconnected from its media file because you've renamed the media file or because it has been moved or because it has been deleted from the computer. If it has just been moved or renamed, it can be relinked to its clip by selecting File > Reconnect Media. If it's completely gone, you can recapture the clip by dragging it into the Log and Capture window.

When a clip is unlinked from its media file after editing, the Timeline denotes the missing shot by "whitening" it. When the shot is played, this unmistakable warning shows in the Canvas. Reconnecting the clip to the media file fixes everything.

As long as you have the FCP project file you can always re-create all your work from source tapes. It is critical to keep project files safe and backed up. Lucky for us this is easy because they are so small. Media files do not need this kind of special care. As important as they are, they are de facto already archived on the source videotape they were captured from. When you are done with media files, you can delete them from your hard drive with reckless abandon.

Creating New Projects

When you create a new project, two actions are kicked into motion: the creation of a project file (which has to be saved somewhere on your hard disk) and the creation of a handful of folders for the media and render files FCP expects to arrive shortly. These all must be strategically placed and named if you expect to find them again easily. If you don't place and name them, FCP will assign them default names and locations—which is fine if you're just starting out, but an organizational problem in the long run.

There are a number of organizational strategies you can use with FCP, each dictated by the particulars of the project you are embarking upon. This is my own quick-and-dirty method of basic organization for personal projects.

1 Select File > New Project.

This will place you in a new, untitled, and unsaved project.

2 Select File > Save Project As.

In the dialog box, navigate to the hard disk where you will keep your media. (Be careful: The default location of these files is in the Documents/Final Cut Pro Documents folder, which can swallow them forever.)

3 Click the New Folder button and name your project folder.

4 Now name your project. The project file will be stored in this new folder.

But you're not done yet. Now you need to establish a pathway from your camera onto your media drives.

1 Select Edit > Preferences.

2 Click on the Scratch Disks tab.

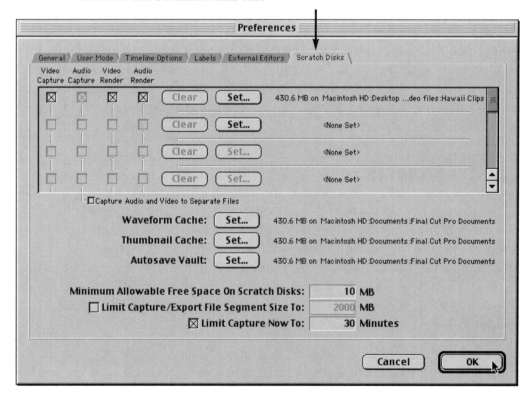

Here you can set the location for three special kinds of media files:

- Video and audio capture files (placed in a folder called "Capture Scratch")

- Video render files (in a folder called "Render Files")

- Audio render files (in a folder called "Audio Render Files")

Now that these are set, when you capture material from DV tape, it will go into the Capture Scratch folder. The clips you work with in the Browser will be linked to the media files in this folder. When you're done with a project, the media files in these three folders can be purged using the Media Manager tools, or, if you're done with everything, you could just drag them to the Trash.

I say three and not four because the default for FCP is to keep video and audio together on the same drives. You can tell it not to, but separating audio from video during capture is not recommended with DV, so keep them together and therefore use only three folders (video and audio both go into the Capture Scratch folder).

As you edit, FCP may need to render effects for you (all the dissolves, composited shots, titles, and the like that we created in Chapter 4). FCP will then automatically create, name (very cryptically), and place the effects in the Render Files folder. Ditto for special sound work that needs sound rendering, although these are placed in the Audio Render Files folder.

Caveat: This is a tidy way to organize everything you need, but as the volume of captured video grows and grows, the disk you have selected may get full. In the Scratch Disks tab there are locations for other disks to be "checked off" so that when one is full, FCP automatically moves on to the next (assuming you have more disks or available partitions). If I expect my video to exceed the space on one disk, I create a similar set of folders on the other drive and set the pathway (as we did in the second part of the above assignment).

Finally, when my project is done, I move it to a special folder of all my finished-and-now-offline projects. I always keep these small, but important, project files safely backed up to protect my work.

Capturing Video

It used to be that getting video into your computer involved actually *digitizing* analog video from tape. The process of digitizing is almost identical to what you do today in FCP when you capture: The video still must be moved in real time from a linear medium (the tape) into the nonlinear medium (the computer's hard disk).

In many ways, capturing video is a little like editing video. You mark source In and Out spots on a length of videotape where there is material you want to keep (in this case, video that you want to have available for editing). If you want to change the In point, you will likely roll the tape to a better spot and mark the new location. This can take a long time, rolling around, shuttling here and there, finding places to mark In and mark Out, and then moving on. (It's not quite as bad as the old linear videotape editing systems, but it's close and it certainly gives you a sense of what editing used to be like.)

The Log and Capture Window

You capture video using a special tool in FCP, a window designed for all of this assistant work: File > Log and Capture.

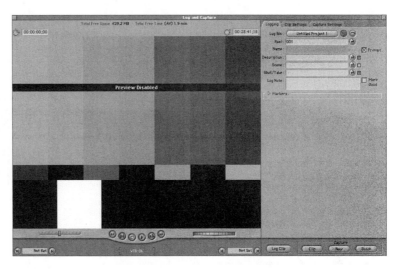

There are a couple key features to this window:

First, on the left are tools for controlling the DV camera that is connected to your Mac. They look like the usual video transport controls, but they aren't simply moving digital files around—this time they're physically controlling the FireWire-connected digital camcorder. Before you can do much in the capturing department, you must make sure your camera is connected and communicating with FCP.

If the system is not hooked up and working property, you'll see this message:

This is a problem. You'll need some additional help if you don't think you should be seeing this. Remember, your camera must be connected via FireWire, and the camera must be turned on set to VCR mode. If you plug in your camera (or turn it on) after launching FCP, and the Log and Capture window says things are not communicating properly, begin troubleshooting by leaving the Log and Capture window, then returning to it. Every time you launch the Log and Capture process, FCP rechecks for the camera ("Initializing Log and Capture").

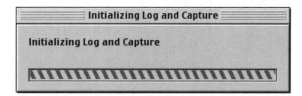

If you close the window and then re-open it and it still isn't giving you control, you could relaunch FCP—but that probably isn't the problem. It could be hardware related (your camera, the cable) or software related (FCP control protocol for this make/model of camera, FCP glitch). As a last resort, restart your Mac with your camera turned on and connected to the Mac with a FireWire cable. If that doesn't work, seek help.

What you want to see is this:

When it says "VTR OK," you should be able to play, pause, and rewind the cassette in the camera using FCP, and the color bars in the preview window will be replaced by video images on the display. You won't be able to see the camera's built-in timecode or datacode displays over the picture in FCP, even if you see them on the LCD of the camera. But the timecode should be visible in the Log and Capture timecode window on the top right above the image.

Even if the timecode is visible on your camera (left), you won't see it during capture in FCP (right). But it's being read, and can always be found in the upper-right timecode display.

Below the video frame is the familiar array of transport controls for play, stop, and so on—the keyboard controls work on the camera as well. There are a couple other buttons in the bottom portion of the left side of the window, but we are going to ignore those for now.

The right side of the window is the metadata center, called the *logging information* by all normal people: It contains reel number, description, notes, and so forth. This data is what FCP knows about a media file. When you organize, search through, or sort clips, you're using the information entered here.

When clips go into the Browser, they're "really" going into the Log Bin—a *conceptual* folder (you can't see it) that we have simply been referring to as the Browser. If you do nothing to change it, clips you put in the Browser are kept at this *root level*. But you can actually create folders in the Browser to help organize material. These folders are also "Log Bins" and you can have bins in bins, if that's the way you want to set things up. On small projects it's unnecessary to use any Log Bin but the root. What you'll see in the metadata side of the Log and Capture window is that the Log Bin is listed—the default being the root level (which it auto-enters as the name of the project).

Loading a Tape and Entering Info

Capturing is about getting the material from the digital tape into the computer. Since FCP can read the timecode on the tape, you're spared the tedious job of typing timecode numbers as part of this capturing process. But there is one piece of data FCP does need you to enter: the reel identification. Everything else is superfluous for the beginner (unless you have the time and inclination).

I harp a lot on this reel number thing. It's so simple, and so important, but because FCP inserts a default number in this field, it's easy to skip. Entering a reel number is the only way to let FCP know what tape you're using. With a reel number and a timecode, FCP can "understand" every shot you use, even if you manipulate it, move it around in the computer, or delete it (and if you delete it, a reel number makes it possible to get it back easily!).

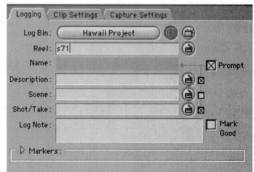

On the left are the default settings for a new project: The project "Untitled" is listed as the Log Bin, and the Reel field reads 001. Compare this to a very simple set-up for capturing—only the Reel field is filled in, and it remains unchanged for the entire tape.

When you eject a tape from your camera, FCP is watching. And when you put a tape back into your camera, FCP sees that too—and prompts you to enter the all-important reel number it suspects has changed.

I do not enter scene or take numbers or any description of the clips I capture. This is because I am editing personal "sketches" with no scripts or slates, and I am

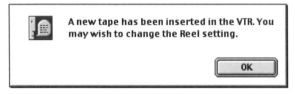

A new tape has been inserted in the VTR. You may wish to change the Reel setting.

OK

capturing every bit of video I shot for a given scene. In the time it would take me to organize this material, make notes, and break it down into small clips, I could have spent an hour actually editing. For me, the first pass at editing a personal sketch is roughly akin to the logging process—finding good bits, moving them around, and knowing what material I have and where it is. I can also add any of this information later if I determine it's necessary. I even name my clip later, as part of the saving process. I don't waste any time entering metadata initially.

With all the necessary information entered, we can move our attention to the buttons on the bottom right. If you really want to streamline the slowest and most tedious part of post-production, you'll capture video in real time—you'll capture it "now."

Capturing Now

FCP has three options for capturing your video: Clip, Now, and Batch.

Clip is how you log and then capture in two short steps. Using the Log and Capture window, you shuttle your videotape around, find where you want a shot to begin (mark an In), roll through it until you see where you want it to end (mark an Out), and then click Clip, which instructs FCP to rewind the tape, grab this media, and stop when it's done.

Clip is best when the quantity of material you want to use from a tape is significantly smaller than the tape as a whole. Say you're shuttling through your tape and you want one shot from right here. Or there are a few 15-second shots on the tape you need to get, but they are separated by large spans of time. Or there's really bad timecode on the tape and you simply must be careful when you capture to miss those broken spots.

Batch is a special (quasi-professional) feature, used when a videotape has been logged somewhere else, or in FCP without having been captured. Batch means you're coming into the capturing process with a list of clips you've marked and saved. Instead of going one at a time (using Clip), this automates the capturing from your "Batch List."

Batch is a must-have feature for pros. I used Batch on all my professional projects, but I've never needed to use either Clip or Batch in my personal projects.

In my book (and this *is* my book), the capture option designed for beginners is **Now**.

When a tape is rolling along, clicking Now starts capturing within a second or three, with no In or Out point selected. With no pre-rolling or cueing up or anything. Just real-time, live grabbing of video. And it won't stop unless you stop it (by pressing the Escape key on the keyboard.)

With even only a vague idea of what is on a tape, and with unbroken timecode, it's very easy to get your video captured into FCP and ready for work. Using Now you can place a 30-minute tape into the computer in about 30 minutes (as compared to 40–60 minutes using other methods).

Then, if you want, the long clip or clips can be divided into *subclips* for easier access. I treat my video in the computer much as if it were video on the linear tape—but with instantaneous random access. For documentary-style projects, I don't know what I need or how I'm going to organize it at the get-go. By capturing long clips, I have that speed and flexibility. It's not right for everybody or every project, but for many, it's ideal.

Warning: When you capture Now there are two things to be aware of. First, there's often a delay between the instant you press Now and the time FCP actually kicks into capture mode. Since your video is playing before you hit the button, there can be a difference of many frames between the time you wanted to start and the moment capturing actually begins—the difference can even be many seconds long! Capture Now is a crude method that assumes you can afford sloppiness. That's one reason I don't start and stop frequently, preferring to grab material in large chunks instead. For more precise capturing, you really have to use the other capture options.

Second, FCP insists on unbroken timecode. If you roll into a zone with no timecode (a break, a discontinuity, a blue gap), you can tell FCP to keep on capturing, but when you stop the capture, it will warn you that the timecode is bad and you should recapture.

If you want to capture from a tape with broken timecode, you'll need to go to Preferences > General and tell FCP not to stop capturing if it sees a break in code.

If you edit with the clip anyway, the software will work, the source timecode will be problematic, and you will have problems if you need to recapture this clip for any reason. I have also sporadically seen glitches in my captured video

> WARNING: A timecode break was encountered while capturing "Untitled 0000". You MUST relog these clips and recapture them without timecode breaks. Timecode breaks will cause all subsequent instances of a clip to have unreliable timecode.
>
> OK

following a break in timecode, including picture and sound running out of sync from each other and the video itself disintegrating into noise and garbage. Capture Now should not be used if your timecode is spotty or sporadic on the source tape—but frankly, you shouldn't be using tapes recorded in this way.

Naming and Saving Clips

Rolling through your video and capturing on the fly using Now will get your media into the Capture Scratch folder, but it's not yet in the Browser and FCP still doesn't know much about it. You need to save the clip first, and you probably should consider a rudimentary system for naming and keeping clips organized. Capture Now *does not save,* the way that Capture Clip and Batch do. Too often, beginners get through the Capture Now process only to discover their clip has "vanished" or isn't to be found in the Browser, where they thought it was going. With Capture Now, saving doesn't happen on its own.

Once a clip has been captured, a new window pops up over the FCP display that contains the clip. It is titled with a default FCP name (usually something like "Untitled 0000") and it is just sitting there.

You can play it if you want to, but the first thing I always do is click on the video and drag it to the Browser. When you let go over the Browser, you start two actions at once. First you will be prompted to name this clip. The name of the media file does not need to be the same as the name of the clip, but it's nice if they match. It makes everything easy to find in case of difficulty.

One problem beginners have is that the Save dialog box often doesn't come up pointing to the Capture Scratch folder for this project. So if you name the clip and just hit Save, the file is copied to who knows where.

If you name the clip first, in the Log and Capture window (before clicking Now), the chance of losing the file on your hard drive evaporates. While it's not obvious, the way you name a clip is to enter text into the Description field; the Name field is automatically updated with this information.

After capture, just do a simple Save, and no dialog box comes up. The clip is saved behind the scenes, in the proper scratch folder. Then you can just drag it to the Browser. Two simple steps. You'll need to see which way works for you.

Once it appears in the Browser, it's ready to use. You managed to save and name the media file and import it as a clip into this project—all in one swift move.

My clip-naming is crude at best. For personal projects—more documentary in style—I try to create as few clips as possible. Consequently, the clip names are simply sequential numbers, like "clip 1" and "clip 2" or "1 clip" and "2 clip" (which makes it easier for the

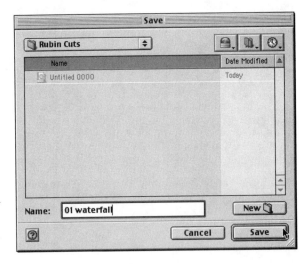

Browser, which sorts alphanumerically, to place the clips in the order they appeared on the tape).

While I might be tempted to name things "good stuff" and "sunrise," these names will sort in ways that may make them harder to find. And since the source clips are long, trying to summarize the contents of each is usually futile.

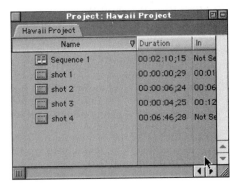

FCP has many sophisticated tools for searching for material, but they are all predicated on entering key information in the

metadata fields—on logging the video in the computer. To find all the shots with a sunset in them, you would first have to have separated all the sunset shots (or marked points within shots) and entered the word "sunset" into the associated description field. While this is good for complex documentaries, it is overkill for short projects.

Anyway, our goal was to keep this work to a minimum. At this point, getting the video into the computer fast so I can start editing is my primary mission.

A Word About Logging

Logging video is the process of annotating a videotape with metadata—information *about* the video. Traditionally, logging can be done on a piece of paper (I love hard copy logsheets); but to be a little more functional, logging can be done in conjunction with FCP, since much of the data you are keeping is part of the data needed when capturing and using video.

Logging captures *no* video, but it does create the clips that eventually end up in the Browser. Whether on paper or in FCP, logging involves saving In (and probably Out) points for a clip. In other words, knowing the timecode values at those points, knowing the tape reel number, and in most cases, assorted text info—like scene number, take number, descriptions, and so on. Realize that you can access all this information and make notes just by watching a videotape on a TV or a camcorder. With a log, FCP can semi-automatically manage the capturing of the video media files and will link them together appropriately.

Professionals need detailed logs. Assistant editors create these logs. Logging takes longer than real time: Depending on the detail of data you want to create, 30 minutes of video could take anywhere from 40–60 minutes to log. And capturing it will take another 40 minutes or so. It's a labor-intensive process and arguably the most important work of an assistant editor. Because an assistant is responsible for being able to find every single shot, the way they are named, labeled, organized, and searched is a top issue for the good assistant.

I keep casual paper logsheets for each tape I shoot (logsheet.pdf in the Extras folder on the enclosed DVD), but I don't spend any time logging into the computer. The shorter my time commitment to the project, the more shortcuts I want to take. Logging is the first to go. I combine the most critical part of logging with the capturing process—getting the reel numbers into FCP for each clip.

Importing Music from CDs

Importing is not really like capturing; it's how you get still images and graphics files into your project, as well as how you extract music from CDs. We imported the tutorial files in Chapter 1. Now we'll go through the simple steps for getting music from a CD in your Mac's disc drive.

1 Select Import > Audio CD File.

If this doesn't take you right to the CD, find it on the desktop and open it.

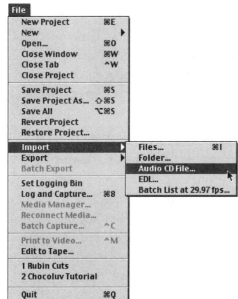

You'll notice that all the songs on the CD are listed as "Track 1," "Track 2," and so forth. So you need to know which song you are looking for before you get to this point.

2 Select the song you want.

3 Click Convert.

You may think that now that you've selected and converted a song, you'll be able to save it. But you're actually still directing FCP to look at the CD in the drive. And since you can't save a file to the CD, the Save option is grayed out. You won't have this option until you change the save location for the music.

4   Use the pull-down menu to find a location on your disk for the saved song. I recommend keeping them near the other media files for your project, although I personally keep a folder called Music, where I always place my imported tunes, and that works, too.

5   Rename the song from "Track *whatever*" to something meaningful.

6   Click Save.

CDs store stereo music in 16-bit format, sampled at 44.1 kHz. FCP's default is to work with digital audio sampled at 48 kHz. Depending on the settings in your project, 44.1 kHz music may need to be rendered in order to play. If your music is at an incompatible sample rate, you'll hear an incessant beeping sound in the track once it's cut into a sequence. If this happens to you, the easiest fix is to render it.

Weird things may happen on your video monitors (flashing blocks and the like) during this import. Not to worry. If it happens it won't affect anything.

Even easier is to start with it already converted to 48 kHz. Use iTunes to import the song from CD, and change its Import Using setting to AIFF Encoder. Choose your song, click the Import button, and you have a 48 kHz AIFF file that can be imported into the FCP Browser.

Technical Issues

You can edit without being much of a gearhead. And because we are all Mac owners, we can run a computer without being too much of a geek either. Apple has made the hardware and software so simple and transparent that you could go through your editing career with an extraordinarily paltry knowledge base, and still enjoy plenty of satisfaction. I put this technical info deep into the book just so no one got freaked out before they really understood how fun editing could be. With some appreciation for editing, you're in a far better place to devote some time to technical topics. You can skip this technical stuff if you want to, but it may make the rest of your editing experiences better in the long run.

The more technical understanding you have, the more confident you'll be learning FCP and experimenting with video on your Mac. Here are my choices for the top technical subject matters to learn a little more about. If you do, you'll significantly extend your ability to use computers and converse in "video":

- Bandwidth
- FireWire
- Storage
- Timecode
- Online/Offline

Bandwidth

No talk of computers goes on very long without the word "bandwidth" coming up. This is true whether the discussion is about professional post-production, personal digital video, or the Internet.

People who describe this stuff often use the bucket-drainpipe analogy: If digital data is water in a bucket, they say, and there is a hole (and pipe) at the bottom that allows you to fill a glass when you want to, bandwidth is the diameter of the pipe. If you have a lot of bandwidth, it doesn't take long to fill a glass. If you have a tiny little straw for a pipe, water is going to dribble out and take a long time to fill your glass—even if the bucket is huge (akin to your hard disk). It's all about the diameter of the pipe.

Every time you see a cable connecting two computer components (a camera and computer, a hard disk drive and the base tower, two computers on the Internet, or whatever), think bandwidth: *How big is the pipe connecting these things?*

Bandwidth, like velocity, is measured in terms of movement over time. For a cable, this is usually described as the number of *bits per second* (bps). For a storage device, like a disk or drive, the bandwidth is described in *bytes* per second, abbreviated Bps (there are eight bits to a byte, as you may have heard). This is also sometimes referred to as a drive's "data transfer rate."

Be careful to note whether you are discussing bytes (Bps) or bits (bps). Many publications and spec sheets confuse the two. When comparing media formats (like miniDV or uncompressed video) you need to make sure all your bandwidths are in the same units.

For more information on these and many more technical and historical aspects of digital editing, I recommend you check out my book *Nonlinear: A Field Guide to Digital Video and Film Editing* or visit www.nonlinear.info on the Web. Shameless self-promotion notwithstanding, it is mildly amusing and widely considered the bible on such topics.

FireWire

FireWire

Background: In the mid-1990s, Apple pioneered a new kind of low-cost digital interface that would integrate the worlds of computers and video. Engineers representing different companies and industries gathered to develop an independent standard that would meet the demands of modern digital video and audio.

The result was officially called "IEEE 1394" (standard number 1394 of the Institute of Electrical and Electronic Engineers), but it's trademarked under the name "FireWire" by Apple (the name recognized by most consumers), and branded as "i.Link" by Sony. By the late 1990s, cameras, computers, and peripheral devices were introduced to professionals and consumers alike. FireWire, i.Link, and IEEE 1394 are all mostly the same. They are all

- A flexible digital interface standard (which addresses the constant signal degradation that occurs in repeated digital-to-analog conversions) that can connect computers to devices, or skip the computer entirely and connect device to device

- Easy-to-use thin cables that have no need for terminators, device IDs, or screws

- A hot-swappable format, unlike SCSI, so devices can be added and removed while the computer is on and active

- Pretty dern fast, supporting data rates of 100 Mbps, 200 Mbps, and 400 Mbps

One key to FireWire's success is that by connecting computer to camera, editing software can actually control the camera directly. This delivers functionality previously only seen with professional editing systems using expensive machine controllers and timecode readers. But even better than that, FireWire delivers true *plug-and-play* experiences: You plug in a simple cable, the software "sees" the camera (or video deck or hard disk) and controls it as required. The development of FireWire was truly revolutionary.

Video, when made digital, creates enormous files. One minute of full broadcast-quality video would constitute a file of around 1.2 GB, and would require a bandwidth of 160 Mbps to play. The DV format (found in your miniDV and Digital8 cameras) compresses this signal, with nominal image degradation. The DV file only takes up 220 MB per minute and requires a bandwidth of 25 Mbps.

What all this means is that the DV format video fits nicely in most personal computers, and easily plays through FireWire cables (25 Mbps is far smaller than the 100 Mbps data rate supported by even the most basic FireWire cable).

Storage

Whether you're talking about your computer's hard drive, a floppy disk, or a DVD, all digital storage media have certain characteristics that define their usability and performance. Because digital video makes for relatively large data files that need to be moved around a lot, two of the most important characteristics to editing are *data transfer rate* and *storage capacity*.

Data transfer rate is how quickly data can be moved on to or off of the disk. It is actually the result of a number of processes. Data transfer rate is important because for video to play, you need to move a great deal of data off the digital storage device very quickly. If you can't move it quickly, you need to make the digital data size of each frame smaller so that you can pump them out at 30 fps. There are, of course, various ways to accomplish this (decrease the frame rate, make each frame image smaller, and so on), but each choice will compromise image quality to some degree.

Storage capacity simply refers to how much data can be stored on the disk. This quantity is expressed in terms of bytes: megabytes (MB), gigabytes (GB), or terabytes (TB).

> After terabytes there are even larger units of measurement. 1,024 TB is a petobyte (PB) and 1,024 petobytes is an exabyte. An exabyte is a quintillion bytes.

New technologies keep increasing the quantity of data that disks can store. Today it's not uncommon for a Mac to come with a 60 or 80 GB drive (with the tower version containing room for three more drives inside the chassis) and with external FireWire devices, you can store even more data. Although a super-large drive seems like a blessing (and it is), there are some technical issues associated with video performance related to this big ol' drive.

In traditional professional systems, it's considered good form to have your application software on one hard disk and your video media on another. In even more demanding situations, professionals often separate the video media from the audio, keeping them on separate hard disks. The goal is to make sure video and audio can be accessed quickly, with minimal opportunity for playback problems. Separating media files from the applications and system files further protects you from risks to your Mac should the digital media files get corrupted somehow and result in a full hard disk repair or replacement. You wouldn't want to wipe out your whole computer simply because a media file was ruined or you felt the need to reformat a drive.

Many professionals I know cannot divorce themselves from the need to maintain these separations. Apple even recommends them for best system performance. The ideal Mac configuration includes a small hard disk with OS, applications, and other files that might be on the computer (say, less than 10 GB and probably under 5 GB), and then one or more large drives for the video media files.

If you only have one hard disk in your Mac and don't expect to purchase another anytime soon, the next best thing is to fake it. Using a hardware utility available on all Macs, you can establish partitions on a single drive, so the Mac thinks it has a number of drives. This gives a little safety margin on your Mac in case of problems, although it doesn't do too much about the performance issues that physically separate drives can often resolve. Doubling up the media files and the rest of the OS and apps all on one drive can result in dropped frames during playback; an irritation that many choose to accept, and others endure unsure of why it's happening. If you're pushed to your limit by incessant "dropped frames during playback" warnings, you can uncheck this setting in the Preferences > General window:

> ☐ Report dropped frames during playback

Mac users from an earlier generation (like me) may still recall when disks wouldn't even work with the Mac OS if they were too large, so you had to partition disks to chunks of around 15 GB. This is no longer the case but a habit that is sometimes hard to break.

I partitioned a 60 GB drive on my G3 running OS 9.2.2 into three uneven parts: a 5 GB part for the OS and apps, and two media "drives" of 30 GB and 25 GB.

For my G4 with an 80 GB drive it was a little more demanding. A 2 GB segment for all the OS 9 apps and OS; a 5 GB segment for OS X and apps; and the balance divided into two media drives (35 GB each). Why divide and not leave them as one 70 GB partition when it isn't required? Safety? Old habit? Symmetry? You'll have to ask my therapist.

Timecode Basics

Timecode is a numbering system used on videotape to identify and locate frames. DV cameras automatically generate this timecode and record it onto blank cassettes at the same time they record pictures. Consumer cameras don't give you a great deal of control over timecode, but the control you have is sufficient, and mastery of timecode is important.

Timecode came from work done with missile tracking for the Defense Department and landed in the world of video in the early 1970s. Timecode is an eight-digit number that uniquely identifies each video frame:

HOURS : MINUTES : SECONDS : FRAMES

01:00:00:00

It works just like a clock, except for the last number, which is frames—each one $1/30$th of a second long.

Drop Frame vs. Non–Drop Frame Timecode

People who work with video often want timecode to do two things: (1) uniquely identify each frame, and (2) give accurate indications of running time (duration). You know that video plays at 30 frames per second (30 fps). Videotape timecodes, therefore, count from frame :00 to frame :29 before rolling over to the next second.

Unfortunately, videotape doesn't really run at precisely 30 fps; it runs at 29.97 fps. So although you can use a timecode number to accurately identify every single video frame with a unique number, this "time" measurement isn't precisely measuring the *real* elapsed time.

Say you've edited a sequence, and began recording it on a timecoded videotape, starting at 01:00:00:00 (called "one hour, straight up").

If the sequence ends exactly at 01:29:00:00, you might be led to believe that your show was precisely 29 minutes long. *This is not correct.* Since your videotape is actually playing slightly slower than real time (0.1 percent slower, to be exact), your actual program duration is almost 2 full seconds longer!

Clearly, regular old timecode doesn't keep track of accurate durations very well—at least not well enough for professional accuracy.

Regular old timecode that has a single number for every frame, which counts from frame :00 to frame :29, and which then rolls over but is temporally inaccurate, is also called *non–drop frame* timecode (NDF), because it never drops any numbers while it is counting.

> Video people never start counting time at zero, they always start at 1 hour. This allows machines to back up ahead of the first edit without running into the beginning of a reel or hitting a part of the tape with no timecode.

The only way to make timecode keep anywhere close to the real elapsed time is to leave out certain numbers. If you skip some numbers (remember that this doesn't affect the video pictures at all; it is only a numbering scheme), your calculations can be *extremely close* to the actual elapsed time of a segment.

Timecode that skips certain timecode numbers is called *drop-frame* timecode (DF). The way it skips numbers is very precise: It drops the :00 and :01 frame number every minute, except for every tenth minute.

This way, source and record times *do* reflect real time, and thus can be used to determine length. (To calculate the length using timecodes, subtract the "in" timecode from the "out" timecode. It can be difficult; you might want to use a special calculator. FCP does this for you automatically.) For the most part, all consumer digital video cameras automatically generate drop-frame timecode—this way, you can easily rely on your durations.

You can tell at a glance if a display of timecode is giving you drop-frame or non–drop frame numbers: non–drop frame timecode uses colons (:) between each set of digits. Drop-frame timecode uses a semicolon (;) between the seconds and frames digits, like this:

```
Drop frame          01:00:00;00

Non-drop frame      01:00:00:00
```

Notice that with DV footage and drop-frame timecode, numbers are skipped (;00, ;01), but the frames of video themselves are unaffected. This kind of timecode keeps better track of the actual elapsed time of video shots.

TCG +00:00:59;28

TCG +00:00:59;29

TCG +00:01:00;02

If you look at the timecode in the windows of FCP, you'll notice they are all drop-frame timecodes. I didn't tell you this before because I didn't want to confuse the issue, but now that you understand the difference, you'll see it more clearly. It's not that FCP can't handle non–drop frame timecode—it can. It's that consumer DV cameras *only* generate DFTC. There's not a darn thing you can do about it.

Online and Offline Editing

Even when videotape editing was first invented, the equipment that managed it was extraordinarily expensive; if you wanted the luxury of time to kick back with your video material and think about the creative choices before you, you needed to use equipment that wasn't so expensive. It was like watching the meter run in a taxi while you edited. And thus the invention of two kinds of editing: a slow creative cheap kind, using lower-quality tools, and a second, expensive kind, less-creative, and using the top-line equipment. They were linked—two sides of one post-production process. The shortest description of these two important terms from the world of videotape editing is as follows:

Online describes a kind of editing (or any post-production work) that results in the production of the final master product (or any *element* of a final project), at an image quality equal to (or higher than) that required for the delivery of the project. The work done online is work that can only be done at the delivery resolutions.

Offline describes post-production work done at lower image quality, for any number of reasons, but principally to save money.

Why do offline at all today? Even though equipment prices for video have dropped tremendously over the years, and the equipment has changed from mostly analog to mostly digital, higher image quality work still tends to require greater resources and cost more than lower image quality work. If you find working at the delivery image resolutions is cost-prohibitive, or simply unfeasible based on the nature of the project (say, dozens of hours of material that doesn't easily fit on your computer), working at offline resolution might be the only trick.

The downside of working offline is that you add an additional task to the end of your edit: You must have the computer re-create all your work (hopefully, without too much trouble) at the online resolution.

In spite of the similarity, "online" and "offline" with regard to video have nothing to do with the Internet or connections to networks. Since this book is about video, I'll alert you specifically if I'm going to use these terms to talk about the Web and related connectivity issues. The primary use of "offline" other than in discussions of image quality is when a clip is "offline" because it's disconnected from its media file.

FCP has, to this point, primarily been an online editing system for people delivering DV-resolution projects. If you needed to edit a higher-than-DV-quality project (for instance, a network television show), you could add a lot of hardware and disk space and pump a boatload more resolution through its pipes, or simply use FCP as an offline editing system. With the release of FCP 3 and its OfflineRT feature, the software allows you to capture and edit DV material at a lower image quality.

DV resolution

Photo JPEG resolution

After you edit offline with OfflineRT PhotoJPEG resolution, FCP can re-create your edits at the higher-quality, standard DV resolution, selectively gathering material from the original DV tapes.

NTSC Video

Everywhere you go in FCP you see the initials N.T.S.C. What is NTSC video and why do you care? The short answer is that it is the video format of television in the United States (and Japan, to name two). NTSC stands for "National Television Standards Committee" and the video they standardized has 525 lines of resolution, playing at 30 frames per second (well, 29.97 actually). Engineers joke that NTSC stands for "Never the Same Color" because there are a number of technical issues with the U.S. standard that make color fidelity difficult to maintain from one device to another.

There are other standards of video. In France they use SECAM. In most of Europe they use PAL video, which comes up often in discussions about video, even in the United States. PAL has 625 lines of resolution playing at 25 frames per second. It won't play on regular American television sets, but provides users with a slightly higher image quality. Also, because PAL is closer to the frame rate of film (24 fps), it is often used as a better video format for eventual transfer to film.

Output and Distribution

As an assistant, you captured quickly, on the fly, with only a reel number in the data fields. Next you slipped on your editor's hat and cut the material as you saw fit, refining it, making a few versions. Then you added music and titles and some basic effects. And now you're done. Here it is, still on the computer, but done. It's time to call the assistant back in to back up your work, master the final sequence to DV tape, and get everything ready for burning a DVD for your friends.

Blacking Tapes

With all this newfound attention on keeping timecode clean and continuous, there is interest in the concept of "blacking" tapes—recording timecode onto the tape before you shoot so that gaps left while shooting do not end up becoming timecode breaks (and headaches) later on.

The crude way to black a tape with a consumer camcorder is simply to record a tape with the lens cap on—shooting "black." Since timecode is recorded along with the video, this does lay down continuous timecode for the length of the tape.

FCP once connected to a camera can do a more elegant job of this: With a new tape in the camera, from the Edit to Tape window, click the Black and Code button.

The question, of course, is whether or not this is good, or even necessary. The subject is open for debate. On one hand it means that whenever you shoot a new DV tape, you are actually re-using an old tape (it makes no difference whether the tape had live video on it from last summer's vacation or pure black, it's still pre-recorded). Consensus is that re-using tapes is not as good as using new tapes.

As for the timecode thing: It's true that blacking tapes will keep the tape from ever having a drop out of timecode. But when you record you will always be reapplying timecode to the tape. Will the two timecode recordings line up perfectly every time? My limited experiments show they do, but I can't say with confidence it will be perfect every time. If they miss by even a frame, there will not be a "break" in timecode, but there will be a discontinuity. It probably doesn't matter much for a personal project (it isn't as bad a problem as a break in timecode), but the effort required to black tapes falls into the "life's too short" category. I tend to skip the work and instead concentrate on keeping my recordings continuous while I shoot.

Why mention this at all? Because when you go to use a master tape, a tape that never is used to shoot video in the field, you can't just start recording from FCP at frame 1 of the tape (actually frame 00:00:00;00). And you can't shuttle down away from the head of the reel and start later, because there's no timecode there. Consequently, before you start recording a master tape you do need to black a cassette, but not an entire one, just a little bit at the head. You can do this with the blacking function, aborting the process after 30 seconds or so. Or you can do what I do, and bump the Record button with the lens cap on. Record nothing for 30 seconds and then stop and rewind the tape. Now you're ready to start your first master tape.

The Master Tape

A project isn't really done until the final video is recorded in its high-quality DV format back to a master videotape. As I mentioned, I use different tapes for source material (that I shoot) and master material (that represents different cuts of the project). And now it's time to get an M tape, label it, and get it in your camera.

1 Label a master tape ("M01," for instance) and insert it into your camera, which is connected to FCP.

2 On the tape cassette itself, make sure the REC LOCK slider is clicked to REC so you can record on the tape. Whenever I pull a master tape from a camera, I always immediately switch the lock to SAVE.

Now you have two methods of getting the video out of FCP and onto a cassette in your camera. There's the easy way, and the harder (but more precise) way. The easy way is pretty good for most personal projects:

3 When your sequence is finished, cut 5–10 seconds of black (slug) at the front and end (this could be a duplicate of your sequence if you're concerned about messing with perfection). It should be in the Viewer at this point.

4 With the camera talking to FCP, press Record on the camera, and then Play in FCP.

5 When the sequence ends and you reach the black slug at the tail, press Stop on the camera. Presto. The video is on the cassette. Of course, you'll want to check the tape to make sure it recorded properly.

This is a quick method of output, but for reasons I can't explain, I tend to be more comfortable with the more methodical and precise Edit to Tape function.

Steps 1 and 2 are the same in the Edit to Tape method, so we'll pick back up at step 3:

3 Select File > Edit to Tape.

This brings up the Edit to Tape control window. Here you can control the tape and select exactly where on the tape you want to record the edited sequence. There are many sophisticated features to this window; we will only cover the core process.

First, let's establish the basic settings for the output recording. At the top of the window are three tabs: Video, Mastering Settings, and Device Settings.

4 Click Mastering Settings and you will see a window where you can establish a basic format of your video output. You can play around with these to your own amusement. Many people enjoy seeing a countdown before their project begins, or want to have a few seconds of color bars, but neither of these are necessary for the amateur's project. I recommend two basic settings: 15 seconds of black before your video begins, and 20 seconds of video after it ends. (Can you use 20 before and 20 after? Of course. Anything less than 10 seconds is probably too little; anything more than 30 is probably too much.) This guarantees that your project is always neatly sandwiched between some useful chunks of black for easy access in the future.

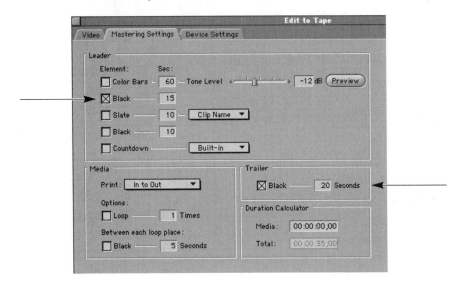

When you're done, go back to the Video tab.

5 Shuttle the tape until you find the frame you want to start on.

You don't know where this tape was left, and you want to be careful not to record over something else. Because you always have 20 seconds of black after your recordings, there is plenty of space to find a clean black frame on which to indicate you want your recording to begin. And because you always begin recording with 20 seconds of black at the head, no matter where you start, you guarantee a clean starting spot. The precise location the video begins is not nearly as important as the rule that it have black ahead of it.

6 When you find a clean black frame to start on, click the Mark In button at the bottom of the window.

Sometimes I like to adjust this record start point by a few frames so it begins at an even ;00 frame, but it's not really important to the process. Because you've got 20 seconds of black before the video program begins, the actual start time of your project (the only start time you really care about) is not going to be at this frame. When I make notes on my logsheet for my master tapes, I use the start frame of the *program*, not this recording.

7 Now that we've established where the video is going on this tape, and we've got our settings right, we need to drag the sequence we want to output from the Browser and drop it in the Edit to Tape window.

Using most consumer cameras you have no option but to do an *assemble* edit when you record to videotape. (I won't go into the difference between *assemble* and *insert* editing on videotape. In most cases, you don't have a choice.) After FCP does a little prep work for you, you will be asked to press Return to start recording.

Recording your master to tape is really the last step in the editing process. With a master version on tape, you can always (later) choose to capture just the cut and do any new things to it you want (shorten it, change titles, compress to some as-yet-unreleased format). When you put it on tape, you've lost the "separation" between shots. It's now just one big clip as opposed to an edited sequence that can be trimmed. This is bad if you really want to re-edit, but it's great if you want to handle your video as a single element, for compression or for inclusion in some other project.

What to Record

In most cases all you really need is the final cut of your project, mastered to this master tape. But coming from a professional background, I have a hard time leaving it at this. I generally record at least one other variation of the project at this time. Because I sometimes revisit projects and want to make some adjustments, I save a version without titles, music or effects—a "titleless master"—on the master tape as well. The edits are the same, but if I want to make small adjustments (tightening only), or change music or titles, this is the video I'd start from. It can be easier than reconstituting the entire project from the source tapes and project files (although that is always an option).

Along with the final cut and the titleless master, I sometimes keep an older version of the cut—usually the first cut—where it's not so much edited as *culled*. This also provides a better starting point should I want to revisit the project, without having to go all the way back to raw footage.

Finally, I sometimes place a final cut on a separate master tape from the one I have been recording on, so I have two copies on separate reels, just in case there is ever a technical problem with one of the tapes. I only do this for very important projects, but it provides some peace of mind when it comes to the vagaries of media in the future.

Of course, when I'm really in a rush, and the project is just for fun, I only make the one final recording and leave it at that. You'll have your own sense of risk and importance of the work you do.

Exporting

Once the video is on the master tape, and before you start deleting media files, you might have a use for a few of FCP's convenient Export options. All of the Export tools let you make some kind of digital file on your hard disk that is built from the work you have done. There are three export options I use often.

- Export > QuickTime > Still Image.

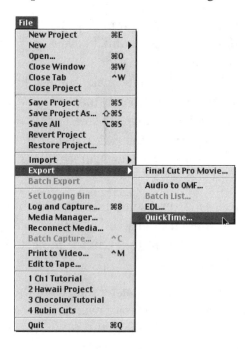

When you are parked on any frame—whether in the Viewer or the Canvas—you can always export this frame in the active window as a photograph, for use on the Web, to mail to friends, to put in books, or whatever. The Still Image option allows you to select the image format (JPEG, TIFF, and so on) and give the frame a name.

First of all, be careful of the default formats. FCP 3 defaults to a PNG image file. If you want a JPEG, TIFF, or some other format, you have to adjust this.

Second, FCP never mentions that the resulting image will be a little distorted from the way it looked in video. If there's any movement in the frame, you'll see distracting scan lines. This is because what you think of as a "frame" of video, is really two "fields" of video (effectively two half frames). When there is very little movement in the frame, this may not pose a problem, but with considerable motion, the two fields may contain very different images and the combined image will look odd. You can make a Still Image of the frame in FCP, apply the De-interlace of Flicker filter to the still image in the Viewer, then export that in the usual way. Or you can export first, then use photo manipulation software (like Adobe Photoshop) to de-interlace these scan lines. Neither method is elegant, but at the same time, neither is that hard.

Before de-interlace

After de-interlace

Another problem is the shape of the video frame. I won't get too technical here, but the pixels in the video on screen are not really square, they're really a little rectangular. So when you export an image file from DV videotape and look at it on a computer (where pixels are square), the 720 x 480–pixel image will get stretched. To compensate for this distortion, your image manipulation software will need to squeeze the image into its original aspect ratio of 4:3, converting a 720 x 480 image into a 640 x 480 image.

Before resizing

After resizing

After de-interlacing and resizing the exported file, it will look about the same as the original video frame.

- Export > FCP Movie ("Make Movie Self-Contained")

This is a convenient feature that outputs the discrete bits of video placed together in edited sequence as a single neat file. The resulting file is virtually indistinguishable from the original video in FCP, because it's an exact bit-for-bit duplicate of the DV data that was on your tape and is in your source media files. Sometimes when I'm finished with a project, I want to keep the final video on my computer even after I toss out all the media files. Creating a self-contained FCP movie is a simple way to do this, although the process takes a little time to execute and the resulting file is large.

- Export > QuickTime

Ultimately, if you want to stream your video on the Internet, email it to a friend, or put it on a disc using iDVD, you need to have a compressed version of your cut. The bandwidth required to play a DV-quality movie is high and the files are large. Compression will decrease the image quality (either a little or a lot depending on the compression scheme and parameters you decide on), but it prepares the video for easy distribution.

To stream on the Internet, you probably want video that has a data rate between 10 and 50 KB per second (a fraction of the approximate 3.6 MB per second you're starting with). FCP has some built-in tools for serious compression, but there are more sophisticated products that are designed only for compressing video (Media 100's Cleaner, for instance, or Cleaner EZ, the light version that is often bundled with FCP). If you're really getting into Web distribution, these are better tools for the job.

Making DVDs

A video DVD is not an archiving format; it is a distribution format. The compression used to make DVDs (MPEG-2) may be remarkable, but it reduces the quality from where you started on DV. The quality decrease is often subtle, and even on a DVD you'll see a video that is comparable to (or better than) VHS tapes. It's just that after spending all that money on a digital camcorder (particularly if you bought a high-quality 3CCD camera), it seems a pity to reduce the quality of your product. In any case, you always want to keep the highest quality master you can (which is why you "finish" your project on DV tape).

With a Mac, there are principally two DVD burning options: iDVD and DVD Studio Pro. DVD Studio Pro offers many professional DVD features, like interactive menus, unlimited numbers of clips within the disk size limit, a wide range of design flexibility, and chapter stops within clips themselves. But I find most of these unnecessary for my personal DVDs (well, chapter stops would be really great). The issue for me is that DVD Studio Pro requires a fundamentally different strategy—you must do the MPEG compression *before* you bring a clip into DVD Studio Pro, for instance; and picture and sound are compressed and manipulated separately. Consequently, I use iDVD for all my disc-making needs. It works very intuitively and is very "drag and drop."

All iDVD requires is that the video dragged to the DVD window be in the QuickTime format—then it will handle the MPEG-2 compression from there. There are three equivalent means to produce a clip in the proper format for use with iDVD.

Method 1: File > Log and Capture

If you've mastered a sequence to a DV tape and it is no longer on your Mac, use the Log and Capture function to bring in the video as a clip. Pay attention to where you save the clip on your hard disk—I make it easy for myself by saving it to the desktop (or to a folder called "DVD Source") when I'm bringing in old material for disc burning. The media file for this clip can be dragged into iDVD.

Sometimes when I bring in an old video, I see a few things I'd like to cut out before burning it as a disc. While I don't want to "re-edit" really, I might want to tweak a title or fade here or there. Once you bring it into FCP and revise it, you have to export it either as an FCP movie or QuickTime—both of which require greater than real time to generate.

Method 2: File > Export > FCP Movie

Exporting as a Final Cut Pro movie is great when the project you're presently working on is already archived to master DV tape. In the Save window you'll have a chance to name the clip, and also to select its quality (Hi Res for DVDs). If you want to keep the movie around on your Mac, even after tossing the media files, make sure to specify that you want the movie to be "self-contained." This is a slow process, and requires adequate disk space for what is effectively a duplicate of much of your media files. It's not really necessary for most DVD needs.

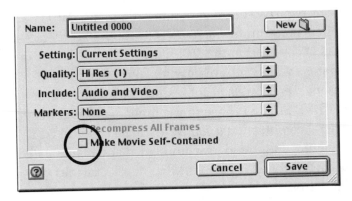

For a much faster and more efficient FCP Movie, unclick the "self-contained" check box to create a Reference Movie. This is a small data file that functions like a single item, but actually consists of pointers to the original media files. It's great for creating DVDs or as the input file for some compression, but lousy if you're trying to deliver video files to someone. Either way, the resulting FCP movie file can be dragged into iDVD.

Method 3: File > Export > QuickTime

Exporting to QuickTime is a little more work because it involves more options, but I use this more often than any of the other choices. The QuickTime format can be used in the greatest range of scenarios. For instance, if you only want to export a portion of your sequence, this method includes the option to export from a mark In to a mark Out. Once your selection is made, go to the Export > QuickTime command, and click Options.

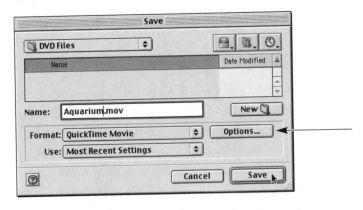

In the Compression Settings window, set Compressor to DV-NTSC and set Quality to Best.

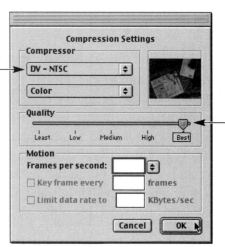

In the Sound Settings window, set Compressor to None, Rate to 48 kHz, and Size to 16-bit stereo.

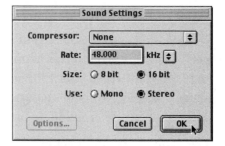

No need to prepare the clip for Internet streaming (not at this size!). You'll generate a DV file that's a subset of your sequence and can be dragged into iDVD.

The specifics of using iDVD or DVD Studio Pro are beyond the purview of this book, but iDVD is so easy that you can probably work it out with little coaching.

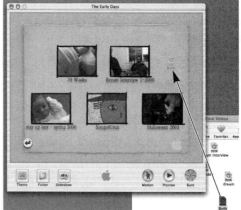

Backing Up

When it's all over, I keep only my project files and throw out everything else. These very small and unassuming files can be used to re-capture all the video from source tapes, they can re-render all the needed render files, and they can be moved from computer to computer with ease. If you've used some still-image or music files, you may want to back those up in the same folder with your project file, since they can't be easily re-captured. Another trick is to drag your Favorites folder from the Effects tab to the project tab before you save your last project version. Otherwise, FCP will lose track of them.

I not only keep a folder on my Mac that holds all my old projects, but I also periodically burn a backup of this folder on CD-R. I burn all of my important personal files now—I used to use Zip disks, which are plenty big, but CD-Rs are convenient these days. However you choose to backup, I'll say only this: *Don't forget to do it.*

Apple has always specialized in keeping the geek-factor to a minimum. Where geeks will want you to talk about your bandwidth, the compression choices you use, and the GHz in your CPU, editors just want to make videos, with as little hassle as possible. Now you know enough to handle both the editing and your own assisting with this agenda in mind.

Professionals, when teaching amateurs, overemphasize all the assistant stuff. Organization is important, and if you have the time, it is something that really should get done. But aside from some rudimentary knowledge and practicing some efficient behaviors, logging and organizing should be kept in check, and editing should get your maximum attention.

All the film school practice in the world is of questionable use when facing the daunting world of shooting a little league game or your family on a beach in Hawaii. So as we leave behind the basics of editing and assisting, let's take one last chapter to see how this knowledge works in new ways when we apply them to the kind of video we often get in the "real world." There we don't often have scripts; we have incomplete coverage; we sometimes face broken timecode; and we still want to make something fun for our boss, or Aunt Phyllis, or ourselves.

CHAPTER 6 # The Real World of Personal Video

Wouldn't it be great if real life were like a movie? I'm not talking about acne-free adolescence and riding-into-the-sunset endings; I'm talking about the way scenes are shot, over and over, until they're right. I'm talking about having great lines of dialog, perfectly lighted scenes, smooth camera moves, and well-planned coverage. This is how movies are made. Editing makes them seem "natural," but the experience in production is anything but.

The tutorial material we worked with was shot in this "movie style"—it had a script and multiple takes and angles. Home video material is considerably more haphazard. Content-wise, home videos are very "POV"—there are no real takes and there is usually incomplete coverage. The real world, the place where I do most of my shooting, happens slowly and sequentially (in "scene order," as it would be called in Hollywood).

Why in Chapter 6 of a book about Final Cut Pro are we talking about shooting? Because editing style depends largely on the source material. Scripted videos lend themselves to a certain kind of organization and a certain kind of editing (the kind we did in prior chapters). Documentaries require a different kind of organization and editing. They defy organization according to scene numbers, and editing probably won't follow a shooting script. In this chapter we'll look at the FCP issues associated with shooting and editing (probably) non-professional projects that are mostly unscripted events.

What's in Your Camera Now?

You will shoot differently once you know how to edit. You won't be able to help yourself. It just becomes intolerable to knowingly shoot the kinds of material that you are certain will be impossible to use while you edit. But you probably have hours of material you've already shot, material that isn't perfect or hasn't benefited from your new editing experience. Is all this material a loss? How do you edit *that* stuff?

I don't want to scare you, but it's going to be challenging.

Let's approach your old material with three topics in mind:

- The timecode: It's probably broken
- Culling vs. editing
- Video slideshows: making a compilation video

Broken Timecode

It's easy to accidentally break the timecode on a tape—to leave a gap (even as short as a frame) between segments of recorded material because you've stopped to watch the tape as you go. Unless you start recording over a part of the tape that already has timecode, when you start shooting anew, the camera will restart counting. A tape with broken timecode (if viewed in a hypothetical timeline) might look like this:

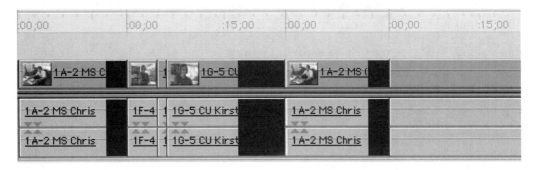

After the recording stops, there's a gap of blue—short or long—and then the video starts again, with the timecode reset to 00:00:00;00. You end up with a bunch of shots on the tape starting at :00;00.

While the timecode will still tell you how long each segment of video runs, it won't tell you the order of segments, that is, whether one comes before or after another. That, you'd have to guess or write down.

If you're dealing with broken timecode on your tape, there are two things you might do: Try to use the tape anyway or try to fix the timecode.

Using the Tape

Using FCP's clip capture functions, you can surgically extract bits of video off a tape with broken timecode. You'll miss a few seconds here and there, but it's not a total loss.

The problem is that if FCP doesn't see timecode on the tape while it's looking for something, it will get lost. You can manually control the camera to stop FCP from scanning in the wrong direction for the frame it's looking for, but you still need to mark In frames and Out frames to capture material in regions of the tape where FCP will not bump into a frame without timecode. This means marking points far enough from the timecode gaps that prerolls will not hit them. And even then you should keep your eye on the camera and capture before something unusual starts to happen.

Fixing the Timecode

If being this careful during the capture process strikes you as more laborious than you'd like, your best alternative is to dub your old source tapes to new tapes, and in the process fix the timecode. Since few of us have two digital cameras sitting around to do a dub (and a special FireWire cable to connect them), I'll tell you how to manage it with one camera and FCP.

As I've said, FCP generally chokes when it comes across a break in timecode on a tape. However, it can continue to capture this video if you give it the right instructions. Under Preferences > General, there is a check box that will allow you to capture even if there's a break in the timecode.

Preferences — General tab

Levels of Undo:	10 actions	☐ Show ToolTips
List Recent Clips:	10 entries	☑ Warn if visibility change deletes render file
Multi-Frame Trim Size:	5 frames	☐ Report dropped frames during playback
☑ Sync Adjust Movies Over:	5 minutes	☐ Abort capture on dropped frames
Real-time Audio Mixing:	8 tracks	☑ Abort capture on timecode break ◀
Audio Playback Quality:	High ⬍	☐ Prompt for settings on New Sequence
		☐ Pen tools can edit locked item overlays
Still/Freeze Duration:	00:00:10:00	☑ Bring all windows to the front on activation
Preview Pre-roll:	00:00:05:00	
Preview Post-roll:	00:00:02:00	☑ Autosave Vault
		Save a copy every: 30 minutes
Thumbnail Cache (Disk):	8192 K	Keep at most: 40 copies per project
Thumbnail Cache (RAM):	512 K	Maximum of: 25 projects
RT Still Cache (RAM):	25 MB	

Cancel OK

Simply go into capture mode starting at the head of the source tape (well, near it anyway—you have no choice but to miss some of the video at the very head), and grab the entire tape as one big file, timecode warts and all. A 60-minute tape requires less than 15 GB of available hard disk space, which is a lot, but usually less than an editing system's minimum configuration.

Minimum Allowable Free Space On Scratch Disks:	10 MB
☐ Limit Capture/Export File Segment Size To:	2000 MB
☒ Limit Capture Now To:	30 Minutes

Cancel OK

For long recordings, make sure you've told FCP that you don't want captures limited to 30 minutes—it's a setting near the bottom of the Scratch Disks tab in Preferences. Be sure to uncheck it.

After you capture it, record it all out onto a new tape. During the recording, the camera generates new timecode, and it will ignore the timecode problems sprinkled throughout the source.

Culling vs. Editing

With only the Razor Blade tool and ripple delete, you can roll through your video material and delete the really bad, unwatchable parts. Dropping weird camera moves, lens cap footage, shots of your feet as you walk, and moments when you didn't realize the camera was recording—all this cutting will make your videos more watchable, but it's not the same as editing. It's called *culling*. Culling is easy and fast, and even if you never want to (or get to) spend too much time in post-production, just culling your videos will make them much, much better.

1 Drop a long clip into the Timeline.

2 Use the Razor Blade tool to chop up the clip into good parts and bad parts.

3 Using ripple delete, remove the bad parts.

Unlike culling, editing is less about deleting bad parts. As you've learned from earlier chapters, editing is about building something interesting from the material you shot. Editing throws out bad video, but it also throws out good video—too much good material is still too much. In the editing process, you have to be a little detached from the production and only use the material you *need* to use.

But there are, of course, hybrids of these activities. Often you *want* to edit your video, but after culling it, there simply isn't enough coverage to make a cohesive story. When your material is more like a series of disconnected moving snapshots, you don't have too many options. In this (common) case, it's enough to cull the video and use a few editing tricks to make the bits flow together, without worrying about story structure.

Compilation Videos: A Moving Slideshow

I define a *compilation video* as a project compiled from lots of little shots tied together with a shared theme—time, location, person, that kind of thing. For example, I've seen compilations with titles like "A Retrospective of Aaron's Life," "Our Vacation in Hawaii," and "Claudette's Wedding."

In a compilation, the editing is not meant to hide the edits between shots as if the viewer were omniscient (as we did in Chocoluv), but simply to connect discrete elements that follow one another. In other words, a slideshow. But a slideshow with moving video instead of static slides and without pauses between slides.

It may look complicated, but it's actually quite simple. Capture all your video for the compilation in FCP, so it's in the Browser as one or maybe as many as four clips.

1 In the order the material was shot, scroll through each clip in the Viewer in real time, and grab the bits that are nice.

Don't let any bit get longer than about 8 seconds.

Mark In, mark Out, insert into the sequence. Picture and sound together.

Even though you presently have inserted shots with both picture and sound, I respectfully suggest forgetting about the sound for the moment. Make edit decisions based only on picture. We'll leave the sound connected to the picture, but we reserve the right to drop it later.

2 Add new shots onto the end of the sequence. Try at first to keep the shots in chronological order.

Once in a while there will be a shot that you strongly feels goes earlier than the order it was shot—for example, an establishing shot of something—of course, feel free to insert it where you think it should go.

If you come across a shot that you think makes a particularly interesting beginning or end, move it to the head or tail of the sequence. The easiest way to do this is by grabbing shots in the Timeline and dragging them where they should go using the swap edit feature.

3 Once you've gone through all your source material, play the sequence with the sound on. You're not listening for a cohesive narrative; you're listening for jarring edits. If you're going to try to use this soundtrack, go through the sound edits one by one and at each one either (1) rolling trim it a little one way or another, (2) add a cross-dissolve in audio, or (3) delete the sound entirely and/or replace weird audio with ambience. The more disjointed the various shots are, the more likely you'll want to drop the production track.

Now, whether you've fixed up the production track or not, it's time to decide if you want to add another pair of audio tracks. For music? For a voiceover? The easiest to do is to add a music track.

4   Get your favorite appropriate CD and grab a song. Drop it in A3/A4.

5   As you watch the project with the music track added, trim the picture cuts to the music's rhythm (maybe on downbeats or in syncopation).

6   If possible, shorten the production (picture and sound) to complete the sequence a second or two before the music ends. (If you don't have a prayer of getting it this short, you *could* add another song.)

> You can easily add a voiceover using the Voice-over tool in FCP 3 (Tools > Voiceover). To record it, either use the microphone on your camera in Camera mode or plug a better-sounding hand-held microphone in to the Mic jack.

This method works pretty well for a quick cut of any project, and it's the best way to approach material shot with little regard to eventual editing— probably like the stuff in your camera right now.

As you gain more and more experience editing, you will think of shots you'd like to have that would have made that video better. Things like establishing shots and reverse shots. As I began to edit personal videos more often, I found I was shooting more editable material, which of course positively affected subsequent videos. These are not professional productions, but qualitatively different from traditional home video. I call these kinds of projects Video Sketches.

Video Sketches

A video sketch is a short personal-video project, about 2–5 minutes long, created through about 1–2 hours of editing. Sketching in video evolved naturally for me through trial-and-error as I edited personal projects. For one thing, the more video source material you are working with at one time, the more difficult post-production becomes (the longer it takes to capture and review the material, the more organization required, and so on). It has been my experience that 15–20 minutes of source material can be thoroughly edited in a couple of hours, which is all the time I ever have for non-paying projects.

Sketches occupy a new place in the media spectrum: somewhere between the non-professional, unwatchable clichés of home video and the professionally produced and edited materials of videographers. Sketches are personal, idiosyncratic, home video/music video/documentary projects, but because they are post-produced, they're far more sophisticated than regular folks ever used to create. The better your post-production tools, the better these personal projects can be with minimal effort. Final Cut Pro—with all its power—is still an ideal editing system for small personal projects.

The Little Digital Video Book covers video sketches in great detail. Here is a brief summary of how to shoot and edit them.

Sketch Shooting

Sketches center primarily on events from your immediate experience. Regardless of how long an event is (a summer vacation, a football game, a baby's birthday party), I have found that you should pace yourself and plan to shoot only 15–20 minutes of video. You might say to yourself, "This event is rare, so I must shoot as much footage as I can and deal with the consequences later," but I promise that the most likely consequence is that you never edit it.

The topics of video sketches may be no different from any other home video—weddings, parties, sports, vacations, events I call "big moments." But the greatest opportunity for sketches is in the more subtle, commonplace episodes of our lives, events I call "small moments."

Making a video is not just "shooting"—it's hunting and collecting certain kinds of video that easily go together. You may not be able to get multiple takes of something, but you can get proper coverage of it.

Also, rather than just shooting whatever's happening, there are some typical kinds of shots I recommend you get:

- The same event in close shots and medium wide

- At least one very wide establishing shot

- Some key moment specially covered with a shot and then a reverse shot (seeing it from the "other side")

- As many insert and cut-away shots as you can easily see. Details of things, without concern for sound: hands, knickknacks, other observers, room highlights, windows, reflections, and shadows. Funny things that catch your attention. But short: rarely more than 5 seconds.

The good news is that real life has an interesting sort of repetitiveness that can be used to your advantage to simulate something like "takes." The more repetitive the activity you're shooting, the more opportunity you have to get good coverage. Whether it's jumping on a trampoline, eating dinner, or going for a walk, even events that don't at first appear repetitive still may be. This allows you to get shots in wide as well as in close or shots from *here* also being seen from *there*.

Another important thing: Don't move the camera. It doesn't have to be mounted on a tripod to be steady, but don't pan or tilt or dolly or track or any of the cool things you see in movies and on television. Those shots are created with people and equipment you don't have and with preparation that is antithetical to the personal video process. If you have a tripod, fine. Use it if you want. But for the most part, shoot all shots with a static and unmoving (and unzooming) camera.

Sketch Editing

I've developed a method for sketch post-production that curtails all but the most essential tasks. Logging is gone. Capturing is always in real time (so you only spend 20 minutes getting video prepped for editing), and the next hour or two is spent cutting. The last 5 minutes is spent mastering the video back onto DV tape.

It isn't difficult to cut 20 minutes of source material down to 2–5 minutes in a single sitting. Some stories you cut may not be overly compelling, but by sheer serendipity (and your growing skill), some of these sketches will be enormously structured and powerful. All my editing time is devoted to the edit itself, with little time spent experimenting with and rendering special effects. Using just the FCP tools and concepts outlined in this book—editing, adding titles and music, and a few transition effects—you can edit a sketch.

For the most part, there are two ways to approach editing. One way I call the *Marble Sculpting Method*—cutting an entire hunk of source video into a sequence and removing bits to make it smaller. This is pretty good for culling, but not for real editing. The other way I call the *Clay Sculpting Method*—adding in bits you like from a source reel and thinking about whether they should go on the end (in the real order they were recorded) or somewhere perhaps more appropriate. The Clay Method is how I approach sketches.

My approach is similar to that for making compilations (above), except I start with better coverage, and consequently there is more work to be done adjusting the way shots cut together. Because sketch source material is shot with something akin to takes, it's a little more like editing scripted material—reviewing all angles on a particular moment and constructing a little "Hollywood look" around them.

Like arranging cards in a poker hand, the cards go in the order they're dealt. But if I see something starting to "happen" early on, I start arranging my hand as I go.

When I see the inserts and reverse shots come up in the source material, since they're often not contiguous with the original (master) shot, I don't cut them in the order they were shot but rather slide them into place, juxtaposed to their "partner" shot.

Since not every moment in your videos will have full coverage, what tends to happen is that there will be a handful of shots assembled snapshot-style, then a segue into the part with good coverage, and then back to snapshots.

Examples from a Short Sketch

Let's examine how these concepts play into editing a real sketch. The event here is my friend Ian and I taking our kids to the Monterey Bay Aquarium. Launch the project called "Sketchwork." In it, you'll find 5 minutes of my unedited sketch video called "VidClip3" on the DVD. It's reasonably typical of home video in most respects. I got the best coverage I could muster while still having fun with my friends and son.

The videotape contains what I would call five "scenes"—locations where I stopped moving and stood still, attempting coverage:

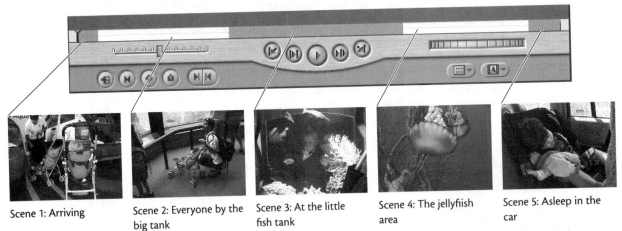

Scene 1: Arriving   Scene 2: Everyone by the big tank   Scene 3: At the little fish tank   Scene 4: The jellyfish area   Scene 5: Asleep in the car

I don't break these into discrete clips, and I don't use FCP's DV Start/Stop Detection tools to mark camera stops. I want to keep them together as they were on the tape. Dragging around in the scrubber, it's easy to find shots. Also, in general, material that will be cut together is relatively close together on the tape. Once in awhile you "steal" from somewhere else, but that's the exception.

If I were simply to cull the 5 minutes down, quickly, I could cut a culled version in about 10 minutes (an example is in the Browser). That would reduce the 5 minutes of home video to a tidier 2:45 minutes. This is fast, involves no rearranging of shots from their shooting order, and loses only most of the camera moves and really long stuff. It's not bad for the time investment, but just a few more minutes can yield much more. Let's look beyond culling to sketch editing.

In order, rolling through the tape, I inserted shots from each scene to tell the story.

1 Something from the parking lot is all that's necessary to establish we're on some kind of road trip with the kids. Just one 3–4 second shot does the trick. Scene 1 is done. (Though I may add a title later.)

2 Now we're inside, at the big tank. Scene 2. If you look at the culled material, you'll notice that material that goes together was not precisely shot in order. It's actually more like a Hollywood film. We watched fish, we started to leave, and then we stopped and watched a little more. This is what allowed me to have better coverage.

If we put shots into the edited sequence as we come across them in the source, we'll always be adding shots to the end of the Timeline.

   Shots added to the end of the sequence in the order they were shot.

3 Now we come to the wider shot of my friends. This should go *before* the close-up of Jonah, since it establishes the scene. So now it's shot 1 of Scene 2.

4 Roll a little farther and you have the shot of the fish (a POV shot). This could go in any number of locations: before the wide shot, between the wide and Jonah, between the two shots of Jonah. There's no wrong choice. You can just pick one, or if you want to take a few more moments, you could try them all and see (ripple insert the POV between any two, then use a swap edit to move it around until you're happy).

This is the process I go through to assemble a first cut of a sketch. In a few moments, the scene is cut:

When I get to the next scene (Scene 3, at the little fish tank), another interesting moment in coverage arises.

As luck would have it, after I shot my son standing at a fish tank, watching the fish (not a particularly good shot, really), he wandered off and showed up a little bit later on the other side of this tank. Without even moving, I was set up for a shot and reverse shot. Neither shot is really very good alone, but together they work, which makes them hard to throw out.

5 So now I can cut back and forth from the front of him to the reverse of him watching the tank. A nice little moment. Not great footage, but excellent coverage, if you know what I mean.

In less than 20 minutes I have a first cut of the entire sketch. Shorter than the culled version and more "watchable."

When the five scenes are cut together, you have built something about 2 minutes long. (See "Editors Cut v1" in the Browser.) I call this the "Editor's Cut," because in Hollywood the editor always starts with a cut of a movie or show, made without much direct input from the director or producers. It's kept true to the script and is the first real cut of the project. Once the editor is done, the director spends some time adjusting bits here and there. Working together, the editor and director refine it, maybe lose whole scenes. When they're done, they have the "Director's Cut."

Up to this point I tend to cut the sketch as I shot it. Now I put my director's cap on and look again. I could leave it intact (and I always keep this version around as family-archives material); but as a director I'm thinking about what is "necessary."

When I revisit the sketch, I'm thinking "2 minutes is too long. Can I get it to 45 seconds or a minute?" and "Can I fit it to this song?"

Making each shot a tiny bit shorter is one way to shorten a project without really cutting out anything. It's not very elegant and it's a fair amount of work.

Smarter, perhaps, is to see if any scenes contain redundant material, or whether whole scenes are even necessary.

I've included in the Browser the first director's cut, "Director Cut 1," where I tightened up each of the fish scenes.

As much as I like Scene 3, perhaps it can be cut out. That may make the remaining parts more interesting. Or maybe there are just too many shots of fish. Video can be pretty and still be pretty boring. I will get rid of some of the back and forth. For comparison, I've also included "Director Cut 2" in the Browser, which is about as tight as I think I would go with this sketch.

I must remind myself often: *You may have to throw out good stuff to make the remaining stuff better.* At this point in the process, it's my mantra.

Approaches to Editing Sketches

The fewer tracks you work with at a time, the faster post-production will be. So by extension, cutting picture alone, with no production sound, is the fastest and easiest approach to a project. It's not right for all projects, but it is a worthy method when first attacking a personal video.

With No Production Sound

If you're willing to lose (or ignore) the sync sound from the shoot, you lose many of the clichés of "home video." Shots can be much, much shorter without paying attention to audio—1 to 2 seconds of a shot might be typical. This is what we just did with the aquarium sketch.

Not using the production sound doesn't mean your video has no sound. It means using either music (which is nice and easy) or ambience (which is more difficult, but not by a lot).

We saw with the Chocoluv tutorial how a dull, scripted scene can be reinvigorated simply by losing the production tracks entirely and replacing them with music.

Music forces your project to a finite duration—the length of the song (3–5 minutes for most tunes). Music lends a structure to the project—the song delivers the story and mood, a beginning and end. And if you pilfered music from a CD, it was likely professionally produced, which gives you a "professional-sounding" soundtrack. Probably nicer than the noise you recorded during the shoot.

On the other hand, the noise you recorded during the shoot is the real sound from the event. After you've cut the picture, you could find long stretches of audio from the shoot, audio that you know will not be "synchronous" with the picture, but still appropriate to the sketch, and cut these into the sound track. It creates a sort of narration track, but a natural one. I recommend starting with one or the other—music or ambient sound—before venturing into a real mix.

Either way, these non–production sound alternatives speed up post-production and increase the overall quality of your personal project.

In the Sketchwork project, you'll find VidClip4, a 1-minute sketch that is an interview with artist James Carl Aschbacher. In it, I used the soundtrack from one shot, and then cut picture-only shots "above" it to be illustrative.

For more on James Carl Aschbacher's mural, visit www.aschbacherart.com.

In this personal sketch, the production sound was initially sacrificed to the editing process, but then added later. The audio track was assembled from material recorded during production, but that does not detract from the fact that it's fundamentally no different from a voiceover added in post-production using FCP voiceover tools.

With Production Sound

When you're cutting picture and sound together, some of your edit decisions will be made based on what you're seeing, and others will be made based on what you're hearing. Because of the documentary nature of most home video, it's likely the sound quality is not very good. There may be lots of ambient noise. Conversations may be hard to hear. Although it may seem more appropriate to leave the sound attached to the pictures and edit as best you can, it will complicate the post-production.

The most common pitfall is looking to make edits when people are not talking, because people tend to speak all the time. There may be no breaks at all, or "speeches" may run on and on and on...and so your shots will just sit there on-screen waiting for people to finish their "lines." If you leave production sound in the project, it will be very hard to shorten the project by very much. And it will probably not be as interesting to watch for those not immediately involved in the shoot.

I cut the Aquarium sketch with production sound on, but without listening to it as I made creative decisions. In my final cut of the sketch ("Director Cut 3"), I added cross dissolves to the audio, did some minor tweaks in the sound track, and just left it with sync production sound (which ends up sounding like ambience).

Revisit the Aquarium sketch in "Director Cut 3" for an example of a project with sync production sound.

Nifty Extras

There are so many wonderful features of FCP that once you've mastered the fundamentals of editing, you could spend another lifetime becoming an expert at sound or effects or any number of other components of FCP. This brief section is designed to introduce you to some of the less-obvious things you can do to make your videos better or more interesting with the editing skills you've learned. All of these "nifty extras" emphasize the "holistic" nature of personal video—the fact that shooting and editing are interrelated, and how you do one directly affects the other.

The Lockdown Shot

Put a camera down on something solid, press the Record button (remotely, if possible), and you get source material that can be edited into an interesting effect. Start and stop the recording, let time pass, and do it again. Or just let the tape roll for an extended period of time—knowing you will edit small bits from the expanse of tape. You're creating a form of time-lapse photography, really, but not quite as scientific. If something is happening on camera, and the camera is locked in its position and does not move *even a smidgen*, you can dissolve from shot to shot and only the stuff that changed between the shots disappears and reappears. This is very cool for shooting temporal projects—an artist creating a painting, for example, or a construction crew erecting a building. The effect you can create is wonderful for highlighting motion against a still backdrop.

Here are a few frames from a creative project: The camera was locked down while some friends and I painted a wall. Real elapsed time was 5 hours. I shot about 20 minutes, and ended up using dissolves between a dozen 5-second shots for a satisfying 1-minute video.

One of my favorite personal videos was a lockdown shot of my son waking up one morning when he was 8 months old. In the Browser is "VidClip5"—12 seconds of footage that illustrates the effectiveness of the lockdown approach.

Although it's ideal if you have a solid tripod, you can use an inexpensive one since it only has to hold still. (Fluid heads—required for any kind of smooth camera motion with a tripod—make tripods particularly expensive. Without that need, any old tripod will usually do, including old ones used only for still-photography. For this kind of shot, I've used the same $50 tripod for 20 years.)

But you don't even need a tripod. You can improvise on any surface as long as it provides a fair view of some scene. I've set cameras down on kitchen counters, parked cars, and stone walls to improvise a lockdown shot. More important is a camera *remote control*, so you don't risk bumping the camera when you start and stop recording.

In FCP, cut in any parts of these shots you want to use to tell your story, and place long (1–3 second) cross dissolves over the transitions. Set it to music. It's a powerful effect—and so simple to execute.

Fixing White Balance

Color correction is a specialty unto itself and is reasonably complicated. But one of the more common problems in non-professional video is poor lighting, and if you haven't mastered the exposure controls on your camera, the problems in post-production will be exacerbated.

While I wouldn't begin to explain all the color correction tools here, I do want to show you how to fix the problem of improper white balance; that is, when you shoot indoors with the camera set up to color balance for sunlight (everything is a little red) or when you shoot outdoors with the camera set to color balance for lightbulbs (everything is a little blue). Regardless, in FCP there is a filter you can apply to correct for the proper "white."

Take the following steps:

1 Go to the Effects tab in the Browser and select Video Filters > Color Correction > Color Corrector 3-way.

2 Drag the Color Corrector 3-way filter to a shot in the Timeline that needs help.

3 Double-click the shot to move it to the Viewer, where you can adjust the settings.

4 Drag the Video tab away from the others (and over the Canvas) so you can see the video as well as the controls in the Color Correction tab.

5 Click the Color Corrector 3-way tab if it's not already visible.

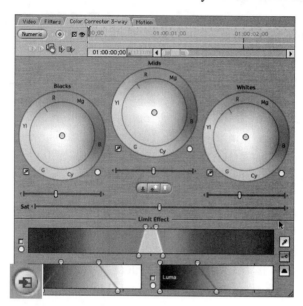

Make sure you're seeing the "visual" display of three circles of color: Blacks, Mids, and Whites. We're dealing with Whites.

6 Click the eyedropper tool adjacent to the Whites color circle.

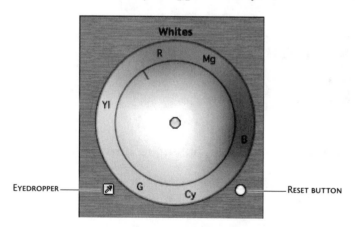

EYEDROPPER ———— RESET BUTTON

7 In the video viewer, find a part of the screen where something should be white (or whiter) but it presently has a blue or reddish cast.

8 Click the eyedropper on this area. You are telling the filter that the selected spot should be readjusted to white. You may need to render. (If you want to return a shot to its original white balance, click the Reset button.)

The Match Frame Button

I can't even begin to describe the many interesting ways you'll use this simple little button in the lower-right corner of the Canvas, but I guarantee you'll come to love it. It really only does one thing, but that one thing is both subtle and powerful. Try this:

1 While you're watching video in the Canvas, press stop, then press the Match Frame button.

2 FCP will find the exact same frame from your source material and put it in the Viewer.

At its simplest, this aids in clip navigation, particularly when you're continually moving back and forth between certain shots. As you progress to more advanced editing tricks, the Match Frame button will repeatedly come into play.

Important note: There's also a Match Frame button in the Viewer, which matches its frame to the Timeline. But since its use is slightly less obvious, and potentially confusing, I'm not going to tell you any more about it.

Contextual Menus

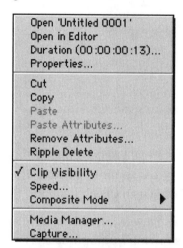

Before we say good-bye, I thought we'd take a quick look at a few of the contextual menus in Final Cut Pro. As in every Mac program, these menus are accessed by holding down the Control key as you click an item or region of the interface. If you're feeling comfortable with the other features we've covered, these may quickly raise you up a notch in speed and efficiency. These are a couple of good ones to examine:

- Click a clip icon in the Timeline for quick access to Cut, Copy, Ripple Delete, and Speed, among other things.

- Click a clip icon in the Browser and you can go directly to Reconnect Media, Export, Item Properties, and more.

There are many contextual menus sprinkled around the FCP interface. Just start small and add them slowly, as you need them. Then when you're ready, spend an afternoon exploring and test them for yourself.

Which brings us to the end of this book. Your understanding of FCP at this point is significant, even if it feels like you've only scratched the surface. You're now in a position to chase down the paths that interest you and see where they lead.

I hope you've discovered that editing, while not that complicated, is an extraordinarily powerful and useful skill to have. FCP makes editing as simple or as complicated as you want to make it. Using editing tools you can

- Cull long videos down into short ones
- Build a semblance of story from the natural randomness of the events you document
- Use video to comment on events simply by playing with the juxtaposition of various shots
- Manipulate sound and video independently if you need to in order to deliver any number of unique result

All of these things can be done with no serious study of color correction or special effects or any number of the features of FCP. Final Cut Pro is a post-production tool—almost a Swiss Army knife of video/audio features that range in importance depending on the time you want to devote to post-producing videos.

Hopefully, this book has delivered to you a foundation for video literacy, arguably as important a set of skills to future generations as typing skills have been to us.

Now go get some video of your own and see what you can do.

Answers to
Chapter 1 Scavenger Hunt

Circle, small, two frames 07;28, 07;29

Triangle, small, one frame 12;22

Circle, large, one frame ....27;09 (*)

Square, small, one frame ....44;11 (*)

Square, small, three frames 49;08, 49;09, 49;10

Triangle, small, three frames 01:07;10-12

Triangle, large, one frame 01:17;22

Circle, small, one frame 01:27;28

Square, large, one frame 01:37;23

Index

C

cables
- analog, 13–14
- coaxial, 15
- FireWire, 11, 12, 212
- S-Video, 14–15

camcorder. *See also* camera
- blacking tapes with, 220
- as component of edit bay, 11

camera
- capturing video from, 28
- connecting
  - to Mac, 11–12
  - to TV, 13–15
  - to VCR, 15
- controlling remotely, 252
- exposure controls, 253
- moving/zooming, 242
- troubleshooting, 198
- using tripod with, 242, 252

Canvas Edit Overlay, 56

Canvas window
- dragging clips onto, 56
- and editing workflow, 22
- Match Frame button, 255
- purpose of, 20, 21
- tabs, 54
- timecode windows, 43, 44, 57

capture files, 190, 195

Capture Now option, 202–204

Capture Scratch folder, 195, 204, 206

capturing video, 196–209
- compared with digitizing/editing, 196
- loading tapes for, 200–201
- Log and Capture features for, 197–200
- Now option *vs.* Clip/Batch, 201–204
- and reel-identification numbers, 200–201

cassette tapes. *See also* tapes
- labeling, 188–189
- logging material on, 9, 191
- naming, 190–191

CD-R media, 232

CDs
- backing up projects on, 232
- importing music from, 208–209

center-point dissolves, 165

checkerboard background, 151

Chocoluv Tutorial
- Dailies Reel for, 51

opening, 52
- script for, 49
- shots/descriptions, 52
- system requirements, 4

chocoluv.pdf, 49

chrominance, 176

clap, 33, 34

clapboard, 49

Cleaner/Cleaner EZ, 228

Clip option, capturing video via, 201–202

Clip Overlays Controller, 128

clips. *See also* shots
- breaking source material into, 51
- defined, 23
- dividing into subclips, 202
- dragging onto Canvas, 56
- icon for, 23
- importing, 28
- labeling, 188–189
- marking In/Out points in, 40–41, 55, 59, 109
- naming, 204–207
- navigating between, 255
- relationship to media files, 192–193
- saving, 204–207
- sliding, 112
- viewing as icons, 137

close-up shots, 50

coaxial cable, 15

colons, in timecodes, 216

color correction, 253–254

Color Corrector 3-way filter, 253–254

compilation videos, 238–240

compositing, 134, 142, 173–175

compression, video, 9–10, 228, 229

Compression Settings window, 231

comps, 142

computer monitors, 12–13

contextual menus, 256–257

Control key, 256

Controls tab, Viewer, 148–149, 155

coverage
- defined, 51
- reviewing, 52–54

cross dissolves, 165, 167–168, 179, 250

cross fades, audio, 130–132

CU, 50

Cue to Head button, 177

culling, 238

Current Timecode display, 44, 57

Custom Layout, 141

T

W

Y

Z